AROUNNA KHOUNNORAJ

Contemporary Patchwork

Techniques in Colour, Surface Design & Sewing

stashBOOKS®

an imprint of C&T Publishing

Text and photography copyright © 2023 by Arounna Khounnoraj

Artwork copyright © 2023 by C&T Publishing, Inc.

PUBLISHER: Amy Barrett-Daffin

CREATIVE DIRECTOR: Gailen Runge

SENIOR EDITOR: Roxane Cerda

EDITOR: Madison Moore

TECHNICAL EDITOR: Linda Johnson

COVER/BOOK DESIGNER: April Mostek

PRODUCTION COORDINATOR: Zinnia Heinzmann

ILLUSTRATOR: Kirstie Pettersen

PHOTOGRAPHY COORDINATOR: Rachel Ackley

PHOTOGRAPHY by Arounna Khounnoraj unless otherwise noted

Published by Stash Books, an imprint of C&T Publishing, Inc., P.O. Box 1456, Lafayette, CA 94549

Library of Congress Cataloging-in-Publication Data

Names: Khounnoraj, Arounna, author.

Title: Contemporary patchwork : techniques in colour, surface design & sewing / Arounna Khounnoraj.

Description: Lafayette : Stash Books, an imprint of C&T Publishing, 2023. | Summary: "Arounna Khounnoraj presents fresh, beautiful entry points into contemporary patchwork with several techniques in fabric design such as dyeing, printmaking with household objects and elements from nature, and painting. Once quilters are ready, they can create stunning patchwork projects, from small quilts to bags and pouches with a one-of-a-kind look-- Provided by publisher.

Identifiers: LCCN 2023025707 | ISBN 9781644033753 (trade paperback) | ISBN 9781644033760 (ebook)

Subjects: LCSH: Patchwork--Patterns. | Quilting--Patterns.

Classification: LCC TT835 .K48 2023 | DDC 746.46/041--dc23/eng/20230705

LC record available at https://lccn.loc.gov/2023025707

Printed in China

10 9 8 7 6 5 4 3 2 1

Dedication

To: John, Liam, and Piper

Acknowledgements

Thank you to everyone at C&T Publishing, especially to Madison Moore,
for being so supportive and helpful in putting this book together.

To all the people who support me and follow my process on social media; my dear friends,
my amazing mum Sengchanh and the Booths—your positive energy makes my every day.

To my children Lliam and Piper: you two are my heart, and I love you both dearly.

A big thank you and lots of love to John for your endless support in life and for
helping me make sense of my words; without you by my side, none of this would
be possible. xx

CONTENTS

INTRODUCTION

As a child, some of my earliest memories are of rummaging through my mum's remnant bin and carefully selecting pieces to sew together. This was my way of practising, not knowing that all those little decisions with scraps and thread were actually lessons about design and composition. As we were a family of immigrants, my mother made many of the things we needed—not just out of necessity, but because of a belief in handwork and the value of making. So, learning the basics—sewing and stitching—came early for me. Over the years, I absorbed many techniques, including embroidery, punch needle, and natural dyeing. But no matter what, piecing together patchwork and stitching was always at the core of what I did.

I remember the moment when the potential of quilting as an art form was confirmed for me. During a trip to New York City in the winter of 2002, by happenstance, I experienced a show of Gee's Bend quilters at the Whitney Museum of American Art. I was amazed at the balance of tradition and artistic freedom, the use of commonplace materials in compositions that were simple, yet complex, bold, and honest. Work that was meant for everyday use and traditionally considered "woman's work" was displayed as art. But, of course, it wasn't just the work that was beautiful; it was that the work encompassed something that we, as makers, all share.

Patchwork, stitching, and quilting have remained an important part of my studio activities. Whether part of my production pieces or as work that is just for myself, they connect me to all the things that I love about working with fabric. They're a place where I can connect with the past, borrow from tradition, and add a few ideas of my own. It's always my hope, in teaching and through books like this, that others will find similar inspiration. I hope you enjoy working through the projects that I have collected here and can use the ideas and thoughts as opportunities for your own creative journey.

How to Use This Book

Quilting has been practised by every culture in the world, each with its own variations, materials, and relationships between compositional structure and decoration. Because of this and its place as a creative evolving art form, it can be daunting to simply define. But for most of us, quilting can be understood by describing some of the core aspects and techniques that form its foundation. Simply put, quilting consists of layers of cloth—typically a front piece and a back piece, with a third layer, such as batting to provide body or warmth, in between. Holding it all together is the stitching, otherwise known as the *quilting*.

Typically, we define quilting by the formal and expressive qualities of the front and the stitching. Traditional quilts come in many different forms. Wholecloth quilts consist of a single piece of fabric, quite often with pronounced or expressive stitching. More often, quilts consist of pieces of fabric, large or small, pieced together to form blocks, patchworks, or patterns. Designs are often geometric, with various degrees of complexity and colour.

In my work, I tend to use traditional quilting techniques, but often in ways that I think of as more modern. My work has fragments and ideas borrowed from tradition and applied in different ways. Sometimes I include quilting stitches and sometimes not. It really depends on the piece that I'm making, and how it will exist as an element of a final project. But what always seems to be present is my fascination with patchwork and appliqué as a form of surface decoration and my preference for working in a free-form manner.

It's not my intention to provide you with a comprehensive approach to quilting in this book, but rather to show you some ideas and thoughts that I have gathered over the years, using the methods and materials that I find most useful. For most of the projects, I invite you to approach them as I do—by interpreting them in your own way. I'm a big believer in working economically (using the materials or colours that you have on hand) and adaptively (by adding your own ideas and choices to each project). In fact, working in this manner incorporates ideals that are common to many quilting traditions. I've always believed in the importance of organic thinking, of how one creative decision leads to another, so I certainly invite you to work in your own way.

That said, I've tried to provide as much guidance as possible. I've included sections on all the basics that you will need to complete each project, as well as to build a base of knowledge that you can use in your future work. I've begun with an overview of the things you'll need to start—tools that I commonly use in my studio, the types of materials that are common to quilting, and a description of the different types of stitching that you may need.

Since many of the projects start by creating different types of patchwork, I've also included instructions for some of the basic techniques that you will need to assemble fabric, including how to piece together fabric and build these pieces into larger compositions, either by hand or on your sewing machine, how to sew appliqué, and ways to finishing your work with binding or simple sewn edges.

All tutorials and projects are provided with step-by-step instructions along with additional notes and suggestions, and corresponding illustrations and photographs. Projects also have accompanying patterns and templates with dimensions that you can use to cut fabric to size and shape, and reference for placement. I tend to use templates in different ways depending on the type of patchwork or appliqué. In some cases I prefer the simplicity of drawing directly onto fabric in a free-form manner to cut out shapes. Sometimes slight variations are fine. In other cases, you might find it preferable to have a template made of paper or card for specific shapes, especially if you plan to create multiples or use it many times over.

With everything in this book, you will certainly be able to find your own way into the beauty of patchwork.

TOOLS AND MATERIALS

Fabric

Choosing the right fabric type usually takes into consideration overall consistency in feel and appearance and whether you will be doing a lot of hand sewing. For these reasons most quilters gravitate to medium or lightweight woven fabric, especially ones that have a tighter weave, which will keep their shape as you piece them together. I usually use a sewing machine when piecing, but I also tend to do a lot of hand sewing on top. For both reasons, I usually don't want a fabric weight that is too heavy. This is especially true when creating seams.

But sometimes you may want to combine different fabrics, weights, or textures for artistic reasons, or just because you love a certain fabric. Be mindful that heavy fabrics may be more difficult to sew, and lighter ones might need an additional backing. For this reason, I tend to reserve more lightweight pieces of fabric for appliqué, where I can use different sewing techniques that will best suit the fabric.

I also use a couple miscellaneous tools that make working with fabric easier: the Wefty weaving tool and a bias maker. The weaving tool allows me to easily weave strips of fabric together, while the bias maker allows me to easily create binding.

Cotton

I tend to use cotton a fair bit, and it's the most commonly used fabric for quilters generally. Because it's woven, it's an easy fabric to work with—it cuts well, keeps its shape without too much stretch, and has a clean surface that takes colour very easily if you're interested in dye. Of course, cotton comes in many weights and thicknesses. Quilting cotton is a medium-weight cotton especially suited for quilts. It is light enough for machine or hand sewing but heavy enough to stand up to everyday use, and it can be found in any colour or pattern.

Linen

I've always loved linen for its colour and the texture created by uneven weaving and slubs. It has a natural appearance that is so lovely all on its own. Although stronger, linen is generally not as tightly woven as cotton, which can lead to issues that you may need to be mindful of. If the weave is too open, fluff from the batting can come through. If the seams are too small, they may unravel and/or create too much wear on neighbouring fabrics. Using prewashed, lighter-weight linens may help, as well as sewing larger hems and adding additional quilting. If you're struggling, you can also simply reserve linen pieces for appliqué.

But for me, any additional work linen requires is well worth it. Combining linen with other fabrics can give your work a beautiful textural quality, and it also dyes well. Naturally dyed linen is one of my favourites. There is really nothing like it!

Cotton/Linen Blends

I have used a lot of fabric made with a cotton and linen blend, and in fact, much of the linen that you may be familiar with are cotton blends. The purpose of blends is to bring out the best of both materials, and that is certainly true for quilting. Blends tend to be softer, slightly less prone to wrinkles, and easier to work with when sewing patchwork than linen on its own. But they also maintain the feel and appearance of linen with a texture that provides dimensionality and subtle changes of colour. Because of this, I find that it's perfect for large expanses of fabric in your work.

Found Fabric

Upcycling found fabric is a good way to be less wasteful, and it can give your work a lovely vintage look. Many older fabrics aren't made any more but are still perfect for quilting. Keep in mind that found fabrics may pose some problems, as they may have different qualities than other fabrics in your project, or unknown qualities altogether. Remember that it's usually easiest to work with fabrics that are reasonably equal in terms of weight. If your found fabrics are quite worn, you may need to support them with additional backing and topstitching.

I love fabric from old button-down shirts and cotton sheets. These fabrics are great for dyeing because the fibres have been worked in, meaning the fabric has been washed numerous times, so it's more porous, as opposed to newer fabric, which tends to have starch in it. The porous quality makes it take on the dye better. Even if a fabric's original prints are faded, it can still look amazing!

Hand-Sewing Needles

One of my favourite things to do is hand sew on top of a quilt—sometimes straight lines of topstitching, and sometimes more decorative work. Some people like using Sashiko needles for running stitches, but I tend to gravitate to shorter needles over a longer size. For me, it's a question of comfort and control, so I use sharp embroidery needles that have a big eye. I find these very versatile for almost any stitching I might do. No matter what you end up choosing, it's best to experiment with different needles to find the one that works best for you. Most needles are not very expensive and easy to find, so it's okay to try different ones. Being comfortable and holding the right size is key since you will be using it for many hours. The size range that I like for embroidery needles is No. 3–9.

Thimbles and Needle Pullers

Thimbles are really useful but also require experimentation to find out which ones fit you the best. I have never been a fan of metal thimbles because they don't seem to stay on my finger all that well. I prefer to use the rubber/silicone types that fit snugly on my finger and have a metal tip for pushing the needle.

Most of the time, I use rubber needle pullers to pull, rather than push, the needle through the fabric. They just seem to suit the way I work better. Also, consider thimble sticker pads that you can stick to your fingers if you don't like wearing a thimble.

Threads

Sewing Threads

There are a lot of thread options on the market, each with its own distinct qualities and uses. There are a few that I find particularly suitable for hand sewing and topstitching, that I use most often. Generally, I prefer cotton thread over synthetics. Polyester is completely usable, but I prefer the matte appearance and natural feel of cotton.

Quilting Threads

Commonly found in sewing stores, the quilting threads that I use are made of cotton. They are a little stronger than standard sewing thread and are sometimes coated with a glaze or wax coating, which makes them easier to glide through layers of fabric. These threads are best for hand sewing. They come in different weights such as 30, 40, and 50 (30 being heavier, 50 being lighter).

For piecing, a finer thread gives you more control, smaller hems, and less bulk than heavier threads. Thread weight for topstitching really comes down to your intention—lighter threads are less visible, while thicker threads are more visible. More often than not, I find a 40 weight quite suitable for almost everything that I might stitch by hand.

PERLE COTTON

In recent years, I have been drawn to perle cotton threads. They do have a slight sheen to them, but they glide nicely through fabric when sewing. Typical sizes are #3, #5, #8, and #12. Again, the larger the number, the lighter the thread. The #12 size is the least noticeable stitch and much thinner than the other sizes. The #3 is the thickest thread and will be the most noticeable if used to topstitch. I like to work with #8 because it's a nice in-between size—visible but not too noticeable. There are a lot of brands out there, like DMC and WonderFil, and I think it's good to experiment to see which one you enjoy using.

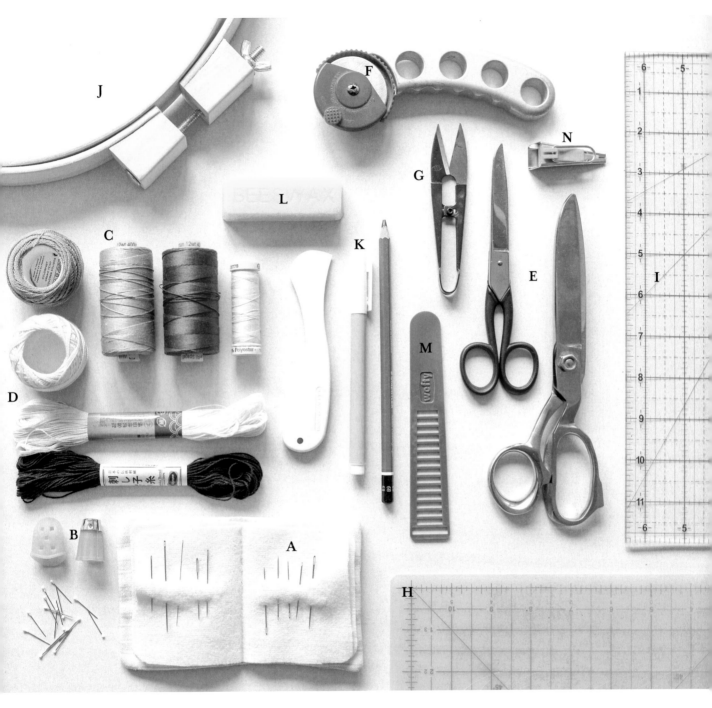

A	Hand-Sewing Needles	E	Scissors	J	Hoop
B	Thimbles and Needle Pullers	F	Rotary Cutter	K	Marking Tools
C	Sewing Threads	G	Thread Snips	L	Beeswax
D	Quilting Threads	H	Cutting Mat	M	Wefty Weaving Tool
		I	Ruler	N	Bias Maker

SASHIKO COTTON

For some projects, I have also used Sashiko threads to do my topstitching. I like the dull appearance, as they have less of a sheen. Like all other threads, they are sold in different gauges, but they are not as tightly spun as perle cotton, so they have a different look. The available colour choice is generally not as large as other types of thread, but if you are okay with the basic colours, it's a good option.

Sewing Machine

While I prefer to do all my topstitching, appliqué, and quilting by hand, I tend to do all my piecing and patching using a sewing machine. Using a sewing machine makes it quicker to complete a project, especially when you have many repeated elements, or if you're like me and you sometimes change your mind about your pieces while you work. If you don't have access to a machine, you can still sew and piece by hand; it will just take a bit longer.

Cutting Tools

Scissors

A good pair of scissors is your most important tool. Cutting accurate pieces is necessary to build patchwork blocks and cut straight lines. I use scissors mostly for finer trimming. Invest in a good pair, and use them for a long time.

Rotary Cutter

Having a rotary cutter on hand is a good way to create quick and precise cuts when used with a ruler and a cutting mat. I find both the regular-size (45mm) and the smaller-size cutters (18mm) are good to have in your tool box. The small size is perfect for cutting curved shapes.

Thread Snips

When I am hand sewing or at my machine, having a small pair of snips at my side is a must. Quickly cutting threads makes things so much easier.

Cutting Mat

A cutting mat is a necessity when using a rotary cutter. And, because they have grids printed onto them, they are a perfect work surface when planning, cutting, and assembling your pieces.

Ruler

I use different types of rulers. I have a small standard one beside me at my sewing machine to measure placement while I sew, and on my cutting table I have larger quilting ones that are made of clear plastic printed with grids. Because quilting entails so much cutting and assembly, I find both types indispensable.

Hoop

It's much easier to hand stitch with all layers properly aligned on a piece that is stretched. But what you need also depends on the scale of your project. Frames to stretch a quilt while working can be quite large or as small as an embroidery hoop. Quilting hoops tend to be a little heavier than embroidery hoops but serve the same purpose. Hoops come in a variety of sizes and consist of an inner and outer ring that hold all the layers taut while you are stitching. I tend to keep my workspace simple, preferring to stitch with my large work flat on a table or sometimes in my hand. But there are times when a hoop is very useful if I want a flatter finished area. To choose the right size, find a hoop that will support the area you are working in, but not so big that it's difficult to hold in your hand.

To stretch the fabric, place the fabric on top of the inner ring and place the outer ring on top, over the fabric. Make sure to tighten the hoop to the point where the fabric has a bit of a bounce to it—don't make it too taut. You can rest the hoop on a table or your arm while you stitch, which makes it easier to concentrate on one area at a time.

Marking Tools

A Hera Marker is my new favourite tool to make a straight line as a guide for hand quilting. Hera Marker tools are similar to folding bones and leave fine creases on the fabric. Simply glide the Hera Marker along the edge of a ruler the distance you want to crease the fabric. Move the ruler and repeat to create parallel creases. These creases help guide you when you are stitching. The marker works well on different fabrics of any colour, and it is easy to change your mind about the placement of stitch lines. To remove the creases, you can spritz the fabric with a little water so that the fibres relax.

Water-soluble markers are also a great way to mark fabric to create a stitch line. These markers work best on light-coloured fabrics and disappear when you apply moisture. You will like using this tool if you find the creases made from a Hera Marker too faint to see.

Tailor's chalk is also a common way to create stitch lines, although I tend to use it the least because I find the marks easily disappear as you touch and handle the fabric while stitching. But it's a good solution for darker fabrics or fabrics that don't crease well.

Paper Card

Having a supply of stiff paper or cardstock is always important to make into patterns and templates or shapes for appliqué. The paper card should be lightweight enough that you can cut it with scissors or (if you want to be more exact) a craft knife, like an X-ACTO. Feel free to use recycled card that you might have around the house; I find chipboard from cereal boxes work perfectly.

Beeswax

While many threads are coated or treated for easy gliding between layers of fabric, some may not be or may roughen up with use. When you are stitching and you want the thread to glide nicely, or to not bunch and knot, using a bit of beeswax can be very helpful. Glide the thread across a piece of beeswax. The friction from pulling the thread will melt the wax and coat the thread.

TECHNIQUES

Stitching and Stitches

Stitching is fundamental to quilting and patchwork. How and where I use different stitching techniques really comes down to the nature of the project. For many of my projects, I use both a sewing machine and hand stitching for different applications. When piecing together fabric into patchwork, I tend to use a sewing machine—it's faster, and the stitches are strong and less visible. Machines are also useful for some topstitching, such as a visible backstitch along the edges of bags. All seam allowances are 1cm (⅜″).

But stitching has a decorative function beyond construction. Hand stitching, in particular, gives any project a certain graphic quality and appearance that sewing machines cannot achieve, especially for visible topstitching. For that reason, I tend to use hand stitching when quilting—adding the stitches that lay across the fabric surface and hold the layers together. I also hand stitch appliqué, typically just going through the top layer using a blind stitch or whipstitch, or perhaps something more decorative.

There are countless types and variations of hand stitches, but there are really only a handful that I typically use. Here are some that will serve as the basic stitches for your quilting and patchwork projects.

Starting and Finishing a Stitch

Most stitches start and finish with a knotted thread. Keeping your knots clean and trimmed is a good thing; remember that when patching or working appliqué, it is easier to hide loose threads on the back, but when quilting, stitching is usually visible on both sides of your work. So, when quilting, start your stitching on one edge where you know it will be covered by edge binding.

If you start quilting in the centre, you can hide the knot within the layers. Bring your needle down into the top layer and batting for a short length and then back out on top. Holding the fabric behind with one hand, pull the thread with your other hand until the knot goes through the hole and into the batting. This will secure the knot and keep it unseen.

QUILTER'S KNOT

Cut a length of thread as long as you need for the project you are working on. For larger projects, I tend to cut about an arm's length.

1. Thread the needle. With two fingers, pinch the tail of the thread against the needle. Then wrap the loose thread around the tip of the needle several times. How many times will determine the size of the knot. *fig A*

2. With one hand holding the needle and the other pinching the wrapped threads, slide the wrapped threads toward the eye of the needle. *fig B*

3. Pull the wraps down over the eye, and continue until you reach the end of the thread. *fig C*

4. At the end of the thread, pull the wraps snugly into a neat knot. *fig D*

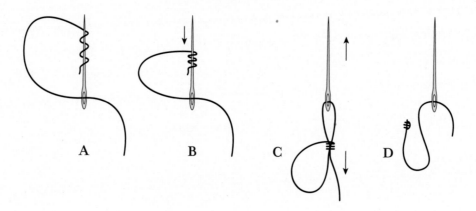

A   B   C   D

FINISHING A STITCH

1. Take your needle under the last stitch, and pull the needle and thread until a loop forms. *figs A–B*

2. Pass the needle through the loop. *fig C*

3. Pull the needle forward until a knot is formed. Repeat Steps 1–2 if you want a larger knot. *fig D*

4. Clip the thread to about 0.5cm (⅕″).

If the knot is in a visible spot, take one additional stitch beyond where you want to stop, and tie a knot. Then insert the needle tip back into the same hole and pull the needle out after about 1cm (⅜″). Give the thread a tug, pulling the knot under the top fabric. Carefully clip the thread.

A

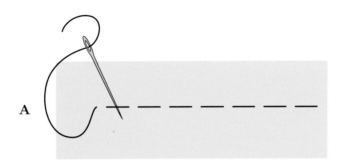

B

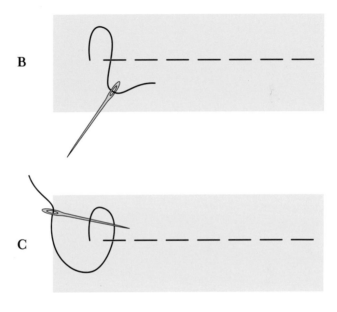

C

D

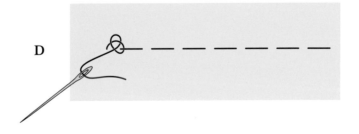

Stitch Directory

RUNNING STITCH

This stitch is one of the most commonly used in hand stitching and quilting. It is simple in appearance, resembling a continuous line of dashes with spaces in between, but the look can be modified by changing the length of the stitch or the spaces.

Cut a length of thread a little longer than the width of your fabric and tie a knot on the end. Starting from below, bring the needle up through the fabric until the knot hits the fabric.

To make a stitch, push the needle back into the fabric the desired distance from the starting point. This is the length of the stitch. Then bring the needle up again a certain distance to create the space. Repeat to create a line of stitches.

The length of the stitch and the space is up to you—I usually make them equal, but changing them can alter the appearance of your project. For faster stitching, *load* stitches onto your needle by pushing only the tip of the needle through the layers of fabric in an under/over movement. You can make a few stitches at a time, depending on the length of your needle, before pulling the needle completely out of the fabric.

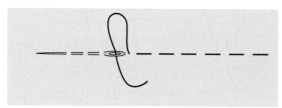

Loading stitches for a running stitch

BACKSTITCH

In a backstitch, the needle alternates between the forward and backward directions, giving your stitches the appearance of a continuous line with little or no space in between the stitches. This is useful when you want a stitch with a stronger linear and graphic quality.

To make a stitch, thread the needle with a length of thread and knot the end. Bring the needle up from below until the knot hits the fabric.

Insert the needle back down into the fabric one stitch length forward, about 0.5cm (1/8″), and then back up one more stitch length forward. At this point, instead of continuing in a forward direction, go backward and push the needle into the fabric at the end of the previous stitch. The stitches will now appear continuous. To continue, with the needle now underneath, bring the needle up two stitches forward and then back down at the end of the previous stitch. Continue two stitches forward underneath and one stitch back on top.

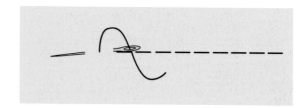

BLIND STITCH/SLIP STITCH

Unlike other stitches, a blind stitch or slip stitch is meant to be as invisible as possible. Blind stitches and slip stitches are very similar and can be used to make hems or to close gaps. I use them when closing openings where a bag has been turned right side out, or to attach a binding or appliqué where I don't want the thread to be visible. In most applications, you will need at least one neatly folded edge so that the stitch can hide within the fold.

To make a stitch, thread the needle with a length of thread and knot the end. Make a fold along the edge of the fabric that you want to attach. Insert the needle into the fold and then out through the crease line.

Insert the needle into the back side of the fabric, only enough to pick up a few threads in a small horizontal stitch. Bring the needle back up close to the edge of the fold, and then insert the needle back into the fold. Slide it forward through the fold about 1cm (⅜"). Repeat by bringing the thread out of the fold, picking up a few threads of the back fabric, and then going back into the fold.

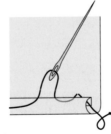

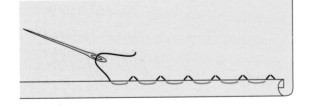

WHIPSTITCH

A whipstitch, like a running stitch, appears as a line of stitches with spaces in between, but the stitches run either at an angle or perpendicular to the stitch line. It can be used anywhere, but I tend to use it along edges of appliqué or when joining layers of fabric together.

To make a stitch, thread the needle with a length of thread and knot the end. Near the edge of the fabric you wish to sew, pull your needle up from the back, going through all the layers of fabric.

On top, make a stitch over the edge at an angle (or perpendicular) to the edge and down into the fabric again. Bring the needle up again through the layers a short distance from the first stitch and repeat. Continue, keeping the distance between your stitches consistent, as well as the stitches uniform in length and angle.

SEED STITCH

A seed stitch is similar to a running stitch, but instead of creating a line, you create a cluster of small stitches. They can be arranged in a random pattern or be organised into patterns, like a grid.

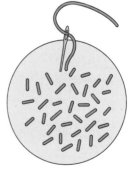

They can be used as a filler stitch, to create texture, or to combine layers.

Binding

An important part of many quilting and sewing projects, binding allows you to neatly finish the edges of projects that have multiple layers of fabric quilted together. Binding not only hides the raw edges of the quilt, but also acts as a design element to frame your work.

A folded binding uses a separate fabric strip folded over the edge of quilted layers of fabric and sewn into place on both sides. It can be used to finish a single side or all around.

Self-bindings use the existing fabric of the quilted piece to finish the edge. For larger pieces, one of the layers, typically the back, is left larger than the other layers and is wrapped around the edge and sewn in place.

For smaller projects, I use a second self-binding technique in which the piece is sewn together while inside out, and then turned right side out to create a sewn edge without any need to wrap fabric around the edge.

Single-Edge Folded Binding

1. Cut a strip of fabric as long as you need. You can sew multiple pieces together if you need a long strip; use two pieces of equal length so the seam is in the middle. The width of the strip will determine the width of the binding. For a 1cm (⅜″), binding you will need a strip about 5cm (2″) wide.

2. Line the binding strip along the edge of the fabric with the good sides facing each other, and pin in place.

3. Sew the binding in place along the entire length with a 1cm (⅜″) seam allowance using a sewing machine.

4. Fold the binding strip up and over the edge to the other side of the piece. Fold the edge one more time so that the raw edge is folded under. Pin in place.

5. Sew down the folded edge of the binding strip using a hand-sewn blind stitch.

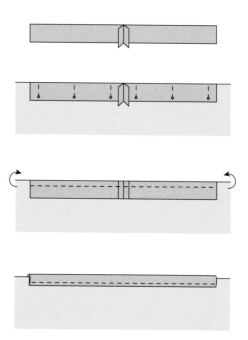

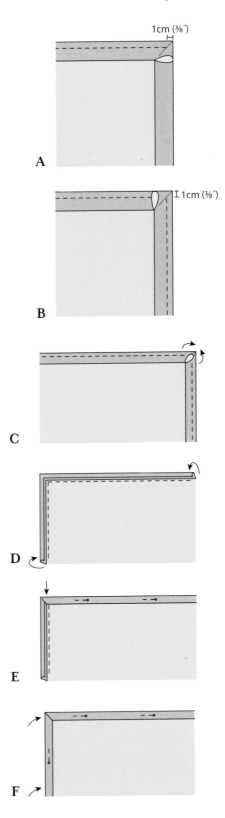

Complete Folded Binding

1. Cut a strip of fabric as long as you need. You will need to sew multiple pieces together so that the strip can go all the way around the quilt with a little to spare. The width of the strip will determine the width of the binding. For a 1cm (⅜″) binding, you will need a strip about 5cm (2″).

2. Fold one of the binding's short ends over to the wrong side 1cm (⅜″), and press. With good sides facing, align the raw edges of the binding to the quilt's raw edge. Pin in place. Start in the middle of the side, and sew along the edge, stopping about 5cm (2″) from the corner. At the corner, fold the binding strip down at a 90° angle to align the strip with the edge of the next side of the quilt. This will create a fold in the binding strip along a 45° line at the corner. Fold the extra fabric at the corner down toward the next side of the quilt, and then finish sewing the first edge, stopping 1cm (⅜″) from the corner. *fig A*

3. Fold the extra fabric back the other way, toward the already sewn side of the quilt, and begin sewing the next edge, starting 1cm (⅜″) from the corner on the other side. Repeat this at all corners as you sew all the way around. To join the ends, overlap the beginning with the end of the binding about 2.5cm (1″), and sew over the previous line of stitching. *fig B*

4. Now that the binding is sewn along the entire perimeter of the front, fold the binding strip up and over the edge to the other side of the piece. Fold the edge one more time so that the raw edge is folded under. Pin in place. *figs C–D*

5. To make a mitred corner on the back, fold the raw edge of the binding strip under in the same manner as the sides. Fold down one side of the strip all the way to the corner; then fold down the other side. A 45° mitred corner will form. Pin in place. *figs E–F*

6. When the entire binding strip is folded over and pinned in place, sew the entire folded edge down using a hand-sewn blind stitch.

Self-Binding: Folding One Layer

For this method, you will be folding the back or front layer to create the binding. Make sure to leave the layer you are folding larger. A front or back layer that is 2.5cm (1″) larger than the other layers will create a 1.2cm (½″) binding.

1 Lay the piece down on a table with the good side facing up. Trim the batting layer to align with the top layer. Do not trim the backing layer. *fig A*

2 Fold the edge of the backing layer over to create a fold with the wrong sides of the backing facing each other. The raw edge of the backing should line up with the raw edges of the top and batting. *fig B*

3 Fold the backing over once more so that the folded edge sits on the top layer. Pin in place all the way around.

4 Sew the entire folded edge of the binding down using a hand-sewn blind stitch/slip stitch. Try to stitch into the top layer only, avoiding the batting below. *fig C*

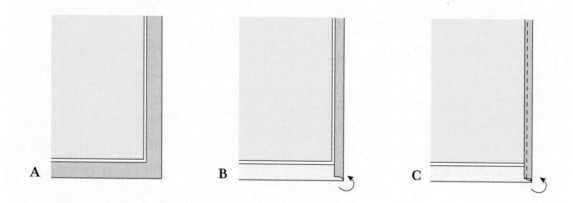

A   B   C

Self-Binding: Sewn Edge

1 Trim the backing fabric and batting to be the same size as the top fabric layer. Lay the backing fabric on top of the front piece with the good sides facing each other. Then place the batting on top of the backing. Pin the layers together. *fig A*

2 Sew around the edge using a 1cm (⅜″) seam allowance, leaving an unsewn opening around 10cm (4″) so you can turn the good sides out. *fig B*

3 Notch the curved seam allowance so that when you turn it right side out, the edges will have a nice curve to them. *fig C*

4 Turn the good sides out through the unsewn gap, and sew the opening closed with a blind stitch (see Stitch Directory, page 20).

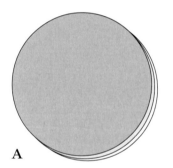

A

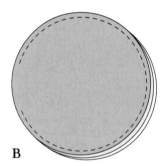

B

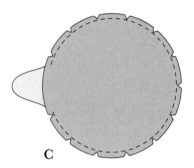

C

Tacking/Basting

Basting is a loose version of a running stitch that is used as a temporary means to keep fabric in position before the placement of permanent stitching. Basting is removed when your project is finished. I use a standard thread and long, diagonal, and parallel running stitches. 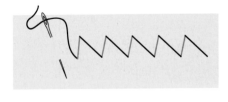 They're fast to lay down and easy to snip when removing. I also use a different colour so that the basting doesn't get confused with any permanent stitching.

Putting Things Together

Piecing is the process of sewing smaller bits of fabric together to form compositions of fabric known as patchworks. It is one of the core aspects of quilting, and there are very few activities I enjoy more. They can be a small part of a project, such as a panel for a pouch or bag, or they can be the main part, such as a quilt front.

Patchworks can be made in a number of ways. My favourite is what might be called "improv" patchwork: sewing together pieces one at a time, making compositional decisions as I go. Determining what colours look good, how big pieces should be, and whether to include other textures or printed images are all on-the-spot decisions. Working organically in this manner allows patchworks to grow as large as I need them to be. The rules of composition and design are up to you: colourful or monochromatic, simple or playful.

Patchworks can also be made according to set patterns, called *blocks*, that are then repeated and sewn together to create larger surfaces. Arranging the blocks in different variations can create different kinds of repeat patterns.

Piecing by Machine

Normally, I do all of my piecing by machine because it is much more convenient. It saves a lot of time, and the stitching is not seen, so it doesn't visually interfere with any other topstitching or quilting. Improv patchworks are free-form in nature, meaning that the sizes and types of fabric are up to you—you don't need to refer to a specific plan. It's a simple process of trimming edges and sewing pieces together.

Improv Patchwork

1. Choose a small piece of fabric. Trim one side so that it has a neat edge. Lay another trimmed piece on top, with the good sides facing each other and the neat edges aligned. Sew together with a 1cm (⅜″) seam allowance.

2. Open up and press the seam flat with your fingers or a folding bone.

3. Lay another piece of fabric on top of the first two, with the good sides facing each other and with an edge aligned. Sew.

4. Repeat Steps 1–3, varying the sizes, colours, and/ or shapes of the pieces of fabric you are attaching. You can also attach complete blocks (pieced previously) to make the patchwork more complex. Finish the patchwork by trimming the edges neatly to the sizes specified for each project.

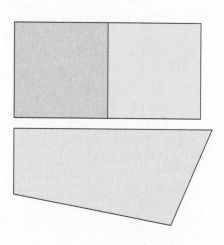

NOTE
For some projects, I will include a pattern to refer to when making your patchwork. But because I'm a firm believer in using whatever fabric you have on hand, treat these patterns as suggestions. In the end, the design is up to you.

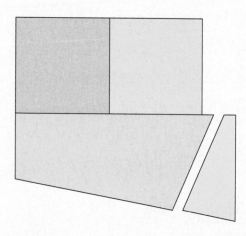

NOTE
Wrong sides are a lighter tint

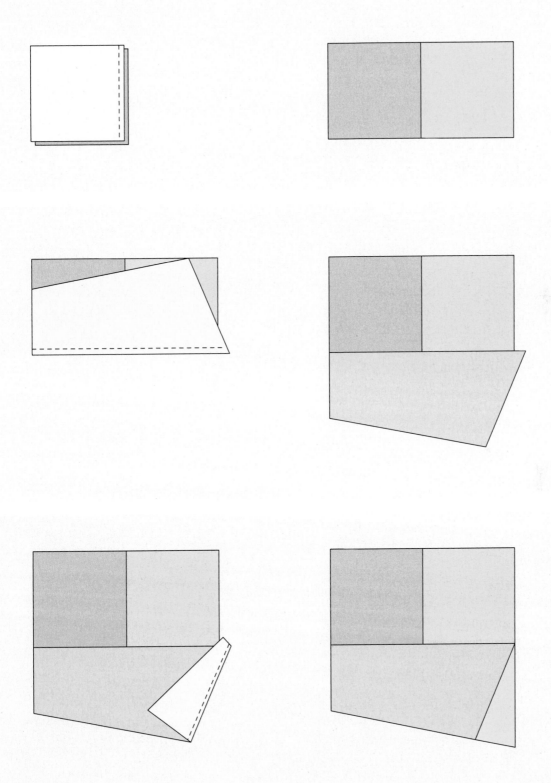

Patching with a Template

Using a template or a measured plan for piecing is useful when creating patchworks of repeat patterns, where you need an identical block several times over, or when you want to replicate a specific design. Measured patterns generally refer to cutting sizes, including any seam allowances. If the shapes for the pattern are simple enough, you can use a clear quilter's ruler and a water-soluble pencil to transfer the pattern directly onto the fabric for cutting.

Other times, for more complex shapes, a template in card stock is useful. You may have to adjust the original pattern to be the correct size, either manually or by using a photocopier, and then transfer it to card stock. A paper card template can then be traced directly onto your fabric for cutting.

Appliqué

Appliqué is a technique in which fabric pieces are applied directly on top of a base cloth and sewn in place around the edges or with quilting. It is a very expressive process and can give you a lot of freedom in your design, allowing for compositions with a variety of shapes, colours, and textures, or even using patterns or images. Appliqué can consist of a single layer of fabric or multiple layers overlapping each other. Edges can be neatly sewn or left raw, and stitching can be hidden or visible.

I prefer to sew by hand when working with appliqué. It's a slow, repetitive process that I find quite meditative. The variations and imperfections that you get from hand-sewn stitches will give your piece a lot of character. Seam allowances are not included for the appliqués, so add 1cm (⅜") around all edges when cutting out an appliqué shape.

Needle-Turn Appliqué

In needle-turn appliqué, the raw edges of a piece of fabric are turned under with the stitching that attaches the fabric to the base cloth. When I stitch down the edge of the fabric, I normally use a blind stitch, but you can also use a whipstitch if you want the stitches to be more noticeable. I also like to use a dark or contrasting thread so that the stitches are more evident as a design element.

If you are working free-form, draw a shape directly onto the appliqué fabric using a water-soluble pencil. If you are working from a pattern with a specific shape, transfer the shape onto the fabric. Add a 1cm (⅜") seam allowance all the way around the shape, and then cut it out of the fabric. Snip into the seam allowance around any curves. *fig A*

TIP: IMAGE TRANSFER

There are a number of ways to transfer an image. One way is to lay your fabric over the correctly sized template, and, with good sides facing up, trace the shape over a window or other light source. Alternatively, make a template made of paper card, and use it to trace onto the good side of the fabric.

If you used a paper card template to trace the shape, place the fabric shape good side down with the template on top (it will appear backward). The seam allowance should be visible all around. Fold the seam allowance over the template with your fingers, and press down to make a creased edge. Pin the appliqué in place on the base fabric with the seam allowances turned under. Sew the appliqué down along the edge using the stitch of your choice (see Stitch Directory, page 20). *fig B*

If you traced the shape without a paper card template, pin the appliqué good side up onto the base fabric. Neatly fold a small area of the seam allowance under and begin stitching along the edge. Continue, folding the seam under with your fingers or the tip of the needle as you stitch. *fig C*

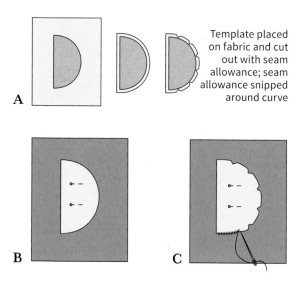

Template placed on fabric and cut out with seam allowance; seam allowance snipped around curve

A

B

C

Quilting/Topstitching

Quilting refers to the topstitching that holds the different layers of fabric and batting together. Quilting is also an important decorative element in any design. Stitching works to create depth and texture within the materials and patchwork of a piece. It can have a quiet presence, or it can work as a strong graphic element. Imagine repetitive straight lines, curvilinear patterns, or even images.

There are many ways to approach quilting. For larger pieces, quilting is often fields of stitching over the entire surface of the piece. I don't always use quilting for smaller patchwork pieces, especially if I don't use batting or if the patchworks are elements in items like bags or pouches. It's a matter of choice. You can also use topstitches to emphasize certain areas, such as appliqué, or to create additional layers of pattern or design. Different stitches or knots can be used for quilting, but like most hand quilters, I tend to use a running stitch. It is versatile and fast since you can load the needle with multiple stitches.

All the patchwork layers should be complete, placed together, and temporarily stabilized before you start quilting. Start by separately pressing the front and back with an iron. Then lay the backing layer, good side down, on a flat clean surface. Lay the batting on top, and then the top layer, good side facing up. All three layers should be visible so that, on all sides, there are equal amounts of batting extending beyond the edges of the top layer and equal amounts of the backing extending beyond the batting.

Next, baste to keep the layers from shifting while you work or puckering while stitching. Start your basting stitches in the centre and move down to one edge and then up to the other, smoothing the layers as you go. Then, from the centre again, baste to the other two sides and then the corners. If you prefer, you can use curved safety pins made for quilting instead of basting stitches. I find the pins to be faster to use, and they can be repositioned if they are in the way.

Running-Stitch Quilting

Using a water-soluble pencil and a ruler, divide the surface of the quilt with guidelines for your stitches. Make little marks for the placement of your stitch lines. I don't always worry if my lines are perfectly straight, but I try to generally space them out evenly and keep them parallel to the edges of the piece. When laying down the marks close to the edge, be mindful of where any edge binding will start, so as not to cover your stitches. Lastly, use a ruler and a creasing tool to actually make continuous lines for your stitches within the evenly marked areas.

Stitch a running stitch along the lines. Start on one end, and complete each stitch line before moving to the next one. Work sequentially and avoid working on separate areas. This will help keep the piece flat and without puckering.

Printing

Prints are no stranger to quilting. Whether store bought or fabric printed in your studio, prints can be used as an overall pattern on your base cloth or within patchwork blocks. I like to use different kinds of prints that I've made myself as accents within my patchworks. No matter how small, they always attract attention, which is why I always hold on to any tiny scrap remnants.

Prints can also be used to amazing effect when using techniques such as weaving to make fabric surfaces. The informal quality of hand printing, with its natural imperfections, gives prints an immediate artisanal look. One of my favourite printing techniques is block printing, which is very easy to do at home.

Block Printing

The tools for block printing are quite simple: a small brayer to roll the ink (a foam roller or brush will be fine, too), a carving tool, ink, and a surface to carve. I like soft linoleum. It has similar qualities to a pencil eraser, so it's easy to carve. Potatoes are also a suitable alternative. The ink will need to be permanent and made for use on fabric. If you don't have access to fabric ink, you can use acrylic paint or any other permanent paint.

Carve the design, cover the block in ink, and print it on the fabric. Repeat as many times as desired. When you are carving your designs, try to keep the shapes simple, without small details—they will be faster to make and clearer to print.

After the printing process, allow the ink to dry. After drying, you need to heat set the fabric so that the printed images don't wash out. I use an iron with no steam on high heat. Place an old piece of fabric on top of the printed surface and iron for two to three minutes on each side.

Transfering Your Design Before Carving

If you're using soft linoleum, draw your design with a soft pencil on a piece of paper at the size you want to carve it. Place it face down on top of the block. Rub the back of the drawing with the back of a spoon. This will transfer the graphite onto the block as a *reversed* image. When you print your image it will appear correct.

For potatoes, cut a potato neatly in half, and blot it dry with a cloth. Draw directly on to the flat surface with a permanent marker. Before you begin carving, you might want to use the marker to indicate which areas are the ones to be removed.

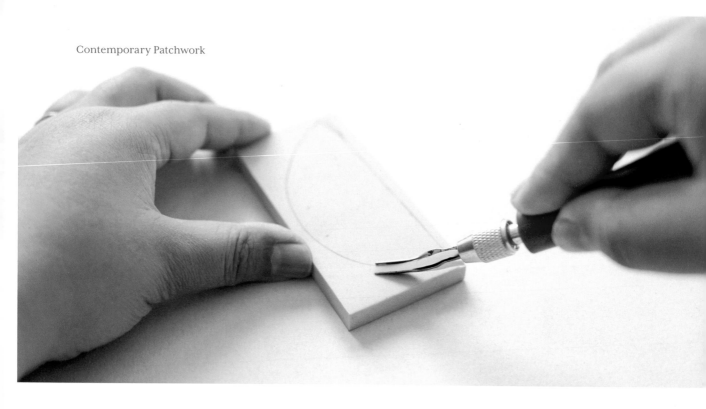

Carving a Block

For the soft linoleum, I use carving tools with removable nibs. I use #2 for the initial carving and #3 to remove larger areas. Use a paring knife to carve a potato.

Keep in mind that the areas you leave raised will be the print. Carefully remove the non print areas. Keep your shapes simple, remembering that even simple shapes, when combined with two or three other shapes and randomly placed, will make interesting patterns. Before you print on your project, do a test print to determine if you have carved the block deep enough.

Printing on Fabric

Prewash the fabric to remove any starch and let it dry. Spread some ink onto a palette or plate, and roll it flat with the roller or brush. Ink the block, using a bit more ink than you might think necessary, so that it can absorb into the cloth.

Make a test print on a similar scrap of fabric. Carefully place the block down and press with your fingers over the entire surface. Review the test; if unexpected areas are printing, go back and remove more material from your block. You can also adjust the amount of ink on your block. When you are happy with the print, start printing on your good fabric. Keep in mind that printing by hand is not a perfect process, and evidence of the hand—blotches or an underprinted area—is okay and should be celebrated. I like the texture this type of printing has on the fabric.

Using Found Objects

If you don't want to carve your own blocks, using found objects can be a good alternative. Pre carved blocks, objects from nature (such as leaves), or household items can make great prints. Even materials and surfaces like bubble wrap, cardboard, or fabric can be cut into shapes that will print interesting patterns and textures. Feel free to experiment and see what different surfaces you like using.

DESIGN

Finding Inspiration

Working in a textile studio, I've always been keen to try as many different techniques and approaches as possible. I enjoy an open-ended approach, where different media can influence one another and sometimes overlap. I find that what interests me is not the differences between different types of textile work but, rather, what all textile work has in common. The materiality, colour, and texture; the methodical nature of stitching; and slowly working with my hands are always parts of the process. So, what I find inspirational about quilting and its various forms of patchwork and appliqué is that I can express what I have always been passionate about: intuitive thinking; accumulating layers of shape, colour, and texture; and using the simplest of means—the stitch—to hold it all together.

So, where do you find inspiration? It starts with knowing what you're passionate about and finding methods that allow you to best express that passion. I have always loved botanical imagery. There is rarely a moment when the shapes and combinations of nature don't find their way into my work. Even when I'm making something that may seem abstract, it still comes down to a relationship of forms, organic shapes, repeated motifs, and the subtle variations that are not unlike what you might see in any garden.

But inspiration doesn't have to always be that specific. Sometimes it's just the feel of a fabric, a way of combining materials, or a colour that just says something to you. Here are a few ideas that have always been useful for me in developing ideas and directions for work.

Creating Mood Boards

Collect ideas and display them for reference. I'm always bringing home botanical samples from walks around the neighbourhood. I have leaves and bits of plants taped to the wall. Real-life objects bring real experiences back to the studio and become direct references for compositions. I also like to collect images of things I see in books or online so I can have a look when I feel I need some inspiration. The same is true for colour and colour combinations, patterns and shapes, and even objects from other disciplines, like jewellery, fashion, and ceramics.

Samplers

Making samples or small prototypes is a good way to see if a pattern will work out before committing to it on a larger scale. Samplers don't always need to be finished pieces; sometimes just glimpses of ideas or combinations of fabric and thread are enough. But, sometimes I do make finished projects, like pouches, so that I can work things out before venturing onto larger pieces. Having these samples on display for reference is always helpful for future pieces.

Drawing and Painting

If I am trying to figure out colours, I look at the fabric I have on hand and use it as reference for coloured paintings in watercolour or gouache. This method allows me to plan out colours so that I can see what arrangements work the best. For some of the projects, I also make multiple painted variations, since how you combine different colour groupings can really change the look of a piece. It's sometimes hard to make a final choice, but having different possibilities in front of you is helpful. Patching and sewing is time consuming, so it's a good idea to do as much planning as possible ahead of time.

Photography

For me, photographing work is really important in a number of ways. I like to chronicle my studio practise by using social media, such as Instagram. Having a visual collection of my work in one place is a good way to see my progress and observe how my ideas grow. It also gives me an opportunity to think of work in new contexts so that it can develop over time. I quite often look back and reimagine older ideas that may not have worked in the past. I find that time away from a piece, and photographic distance, can bring new ideas to fresh eyes.

Planning Designs

Composition

There are a number of different ways to work. If a project consists of a specific pattern or composition of forms, such as botanical elements that need to fit together, I tend to develop the design on paper. For other projects that are more free-form in nature, I will skip the preliminary work and move straight to working with fabric.

In either case, eventually, most decisions are made when working with the fabric. I like to compose designs by laying full-size fabric pieces, remnants, or scraps on the surface of the base cloth. It's not unlike collage or drawing. I love the immediacy of it and the importance of thinking with my hands. It's also organic—I can watch the piece develop with the randomness of found shapes and happenstance relationships.

Once the composition is finalized, record the positions by drawing on the base cloth with a water-soluble pencil or by taking a photo or drawing a sketch. Then appliqué or piece your design.

Creating a Colour Story

Everybody has their favourite colours or combinations. There are certain colours that I gravitate toward, colours that I identify with and that hold a certain place in my larger life—the clothes I wear, my possessions, or even my home. Choosing colours that you are comfortable with is a good starting point. But I don't always choose colours just because I like them. In the end, *all* colours have something likable about them. So, I look for colours that work well with each other, and create a story. There are no definitive rules for doing this, but sometimes the key is to give yourself limitations—working with just a few colours and assigning them specific roles.

Consider the project as a whole. Are you working on a patchwork that is a small part within a larger project, such as a decorative panel on a bag, or does the patchwork encompass the entire piece, like a large quilt? I find more colour freedom with smaller pieces, where patchwork is in combination with plain fabric. Those compositions tend to be more abstract, so I can use a greater range of brighter colours, greater contrasts, and even varieties of prints and patterns because they play a decorative role within a piece. I usually have ample piles of remnants when patching, so I try different combinations as I go, seeing if one colour works, and if not, using another. It's always nice to use some commonalities—using all linens, for instance—to unify even an eclectic patchwork.

When working on larger pieces, I find that I am more dependent on planning before I start working, although planning is not always perfect, because we all change our minds sometimes. But, as a general rule, I find that developing the composition, fabric choices, and colour palette ahead of time is necessary. I tend to reduce the number of colours and plan them with a common element, like colour temperature or colour value. I find these limitations especially preferential when my design includes pictorial elements, like repeated botanical elements, so the simplicity of colour allows me to emphasize the other aspects of the design, like line, shape, material, and stitching.

COLOUR

Selecting a Palette

Colour is a key element in any textile project, especially for quilting and patchwork.

We've all seen countless examples of quilts that approach colour in many different ways. Some are full of colour; others are monotone; others are light, dark, or a mix of both. All of this suggests to me that there really aren't any hard and fast rules and that colour choices are quite often informed by subjectivity. And that's okay!

A typical project for me may only need a handful of different colours, so the key is to find a way to reduce the possibilities down to a well-chosen few. I've found it useful to think of colours as families. A family is a few colours that have a range of differences: one main colour, one a little lighter, one a little darker, and a couple that are variations. But families also have a common element, something that makes them suitable for each other; a good example is my love of the muted colours that come from natural dyes. You can produce a wide range of colours, but they all share an earthy, almost neutral palette.

It only takes a couple of colours to play with fabric swatches and make a lovely palette. Your selection doesn't have to be large—in fact, a reduced palette is sometimes preferable. But don't underestimate the value of an exception: the accent colour that stands out on its own. Colours that don't follow the rules can create a visual spark and speak of the unexpected qualities of the handmade. How an accent colour stands out is very important, and it really plays into the intent of the designs. Bold colour differences and contrasts increase the graphic qualities of a design, while subtle variations imply a softer, more minimal appeal.

When I choose colours, I want a balance of contrast and similarities. Establish a dominant colour theme by using one colour, variations of that colour, and a variety of lights and darks. This will result in unity that has complexity and depth that avoids flatness.

Colour Terms

To help when selecting colours, let's think about the basic ways they are organized. Most colour wheel charts simplify the number and combinations of colour, which helps eliminate some of the millions we would otherwise contend with. These charts give us some useful colour relationships:

Primary Colours: Red, yellow and blue.

Secondary Colours: Purple, green, and orange. Mixed by combining primary colours.

Tertiary Colours: An array of hues mixed by combining a primary colour and a secondary colour.

The word for a colour in its purest form is *hue*. The majority of colours that surround us in life are not pure hues, but tints, shades, and tones—the endless variations that result from pure colours being mixed with white, black, or grey. Hues mixed with white give us *tints*. Hues mixed with black give us *shades*. Hues mixed with grey give us *tones*.

Natural Dyes

Natural dyes are colourants that come from the natural world. While they may include animal or mineral sources, the vast majority are plant based and were used to colour textiles, among other things, for millennia, until synthetic dyes were invented during the Industrial Revolution of the mid-19th century. When combined with certain natural additives, natural dyes have richness and complexity that results in a wide range of variations, surface qualities, and depth of colour which can make them preferable to synthetic dye for artists and traditional makers. Many natural dyes are derived from common sources in our environment and even in our kitchen pantry.

Found and Foraged Dye Sources

Some textile shops carry a number of natural dyes that are ready to be used at home. But I find that foraging what you have in your garden, community, or kitchen is equally good, with sometimes incredibly surprising results.

AVOCADOS

You can dye with the pits or the skin of the avocado. You can also freeze them until you're ready to use them. Avocados on their own produce a pinkish/salmon colour. Fewer avocados will result in a lighter colour; a few more, a darker colour. In addition, modifiers such as calcium, soda, or vinegar can be added to alter the pH level. These will take the avocado pink into another realm of warm darks and lights.

ONION SKINS

Both red and yellow onion skins work well for dye. They can be easily stored until you're ready to use them since they are a dry ingredient. You get a range of yellows, from pale and bright to a darker, almost mustard colour. They can be used to make a dye bath or to direct dye a piece of fabric.

WALNUTS

Walnut seeds are plentiful in the fall around many parts of North America. You just need to boil the nuts in order to extract colour. The resulting dye is medium to dark brown that, if combined with iron (ferrous sulfate), will become almost black in colour.

TEAS AND COFFEES

A variety of dark teas and coffees can be used to dye fabric in a range of browns. The more tea bags you add to the dye bath, the darker the dye will be. This is a good way to use up old tea bags. Similarly, the stronger the coffee, the stronger the dye bath.

LEAVES AND FLOWERS

It's fun to experiment with leaves and flowers and see what colours they yield. The best way to learn from this process is to experiment. Leaves that have a high content of tannin (like sumac, oak, and maple) work in getting a variety of rich colour. Flowers like marigold, weld, and coreopsis will give you bright and long-lasting colours.

Store-Bought Dye Sources

Working with store-bought dyes is definitely more convenient if you don't have access to a garden or if you want to try dye sources that are not in your kitchen. Using dyes that have already been extracted will yield a more predictable colour and help with consistency if you're working on dyeing larger batches of fabric.

Scouring Fabric

The first step in preparing textiles prior to mordanting (see below) and dyeing is to scour the fabric. This is a process of cleaning that removes any natural impurities or additives such as oils, dirt, or starches and makes the fibres more absorbent for dyeing. There are specific soaps or additives that best suit different types of fibres, but all scouring processes involve soaking the fibres in a prepared bath with hot water for about 30 minutes and rinsing before moving on to mordanting.

Mordanting Fabric

The process of mordanting fabrics helps to make natural dyes more colourfast, meaning that the colour will last longer without fading. Mordanting should be done before dyeing. There are many mordants that you can use, depending on the kind of fabric you're using. The most common are tannins, iron, and alum. Typically, fabric will be soaked in a hot bath with a mordant for one to two hours, and then sometimes left to cool in the bath for up to 24 hours, before rinsing. Research which kind of mordant will be best for your fibre and dye.

Mordants can also alter the natural dye colour and intensity. Using alum will result in a brighter colour, while tannin or iron will generally darken the end result. Some dyestuffs, mostly those that come from woody sources (bark, alder cones, avocado stones, and so on), have natural tannins, so fabrics that will be dyed with these materials don't need to be mordanted first.

I also enjoy using soy milk as a mordant. Soak the fabric for a day, and let it dry and cure for three to five days. You can also thicken the soy milk with guar gum to create a paste, which then can be painted onto fabric in patterns before being left to cure (see Throw Quilt, page 58).

Other Dye Materials

Setting up a dye kitchen is quite easy—all you need is some commonplace kitchen tools designated solely for dyeing and not to be used for food. A large metal pot with a lid that can fit the fabric will be your main tool; 8- or 10-quart (8.8- or 11-litre) stainless steel is best. You can use aluminium, but it may affect the resulting colours. A steaming basket to fit inside is definitely a bonus tool, but it's not

required. You will also need a small assortment of long-handled spoons for stirring, long metal tongs, oven mitts, and measuring devices such as spoons, cups, a thermometer, and a scale for measuring ingredients. And of course, you need a heat source; I use an electric countertop burner with two elements so that I can dye in a well-ventilated space in my studio.

There is also safety equipment to consider. While natural dyes sound harmless, fumes and powders can be irritating to the skin, eyes, or lungs. Working with a mask and gloves is always advisable.

Dye Process

Once fabric has been mordanted, it is ready to dye. There are many processes for dyeing, depending on the type of fabric and the dyestuff that you are using. In most cases, the first step is to create a dye bath by extracting colour from whatever dyestuff you are using. Combine the dyestuff with twice as much water and simmer for a minimum of two hours. Some dyestuffs may be more delicate, and may not require as much heat or extraction time. Strain out all the solids, leaving only the dyebath. Lastly, add your wet fabric to the dye bath and simmer for another couple of hours.

Steam Printing/Direct Dyeing

Other types of dyeing do not need a dye bath. In some cases, colour can be transferred by direct contact between the fabric and dyestuff. This usually works best with plant matter such as leaves or petals. Spread the plant material over the surface of the fabric, tightly roll it up, on a dowel rod if needed, and bind it with string. Then steam it over boiling water. The time needed depends on the dyestuff.

Solar dyeing or solar printing uses exposure to the sun to create coloured patterns. By adding soy milk to a mixture with procion dye (a synthetic dye), the soymilk darkens the colour when exposed to direct sunlight. Placing objects directly onto the surface of the fabric acts as a resist to the effects of the soy/dye mixture, remaining lighter in colour and resulting in a patterning effect.

After Dyeing

Wash the fabric with a pH-neutral eco-friendly detergent and line dry. It's also best to keep naturally dyed fabric from long exposures to the sun, which will make the colours fade.

Wholecloth Throw Quilt

FINISHED QUILT: 127 × 152cm (50″ × 60″)

This project uses a combination of natural dye and stitching to make a wholecloth quilt. Stitches are a great way to highlight underlying shapes and forms. I am especially fond of botanical imagery, so I wanted to create a repeat motif using leaf and floral elements that would give the throw a real graphic presence.

In the initial dyeing process, I use soy milk to darken the botanical design. The parts of the fabric not treated with soy milk stay lighter. I used avocado pits to create the lovely pink colour, but you can also achieve a variety of colours and tones by using other natural dye sources. To learn more about dyes and gather the appropriate dyeing tools, see Natural Dyes (page 50).

This quilt is finished with a self-binding technique that is topstitched, which gives the piece a nice border frame.

FABRIC

White woven cotton fabric: 137.2 × 160cm (54″ × 63″)

Fabric rectangle (back of quilt): 137.2 × 160cm (54″ × 63″)

Low-loft cotton batting: 137.2 × 160cm (54″ × 63″)

DYE MATERIALS

4 tablespoons (60mL) soy milk

¼ to 1 teaspoon (1mL to 5mL) guar gum

Avocado dye: I used 10 large pits—more pits will result in a stronger pink, and fewer pits will result in a paler colour

Dye tools: large stainless-steel pot, stirring sticks, tongs, safety wear

ADDITIONAL MATERIALS

Clover water-soluble marker

Paper

Masking tape

Round paint brush, large

Safety pins

Hand-sewing needle

WonderFil spaghetti colour SP18

Notes on Materials

For this process, you will add guar gum to soy milk in order to thicken it. I only used about ¼ teaspoon (1mL) of guar gum in my soy milk mixture in order to keep it on the thin side. It needs to be thin enough that you can still brush it on, but thick enough that it won't run freely. Before you start working with the fabric, use paper to draw out the design. You can also create a paper template of the design to transfer to the fabric. Draw it to size, and place it on top of the fabric, or draw the design small and move it across the fabric to create a repeat pattern.

If you'd like to use black tea instead of avocado for a browner hue, use about four tea bags for a cloth this size. Neither avocado dye nor black tea dye needs a mordant to make the fabric hold the colour because they contain natural tannins. But if you choose a different dye, be aware that you may need to use a mordant. See Mordanting Fabric (page 52) for more information.

Prepare the Fabric

1. Scour the front piece of fabric (see Scouring Fabric, page 52). While the fabric dries, finalize your design and create a paper template.

2. Once the fabric dries, place it over the template and transfer the design to the fabric with a water-soluble marker. Place the fabric over a window or other light source to make transferring easier. If you don't want a preplanned design for the quilt, skip this step.

3. Mix a tiny bit of guar gum, about ¼ teaspoon (1mL), into the soy milk. It should thicken to a

yoghurt-like consistency. Try painting the mixture on a piece of scrap fabric to make sure it's the right thickness—not thick enough to be clumpy, but not so thin that it bleeds across the whole cloth.

4. Paint the design onto the cloth with the soy milk mixture. If you skipped Step 2, paint random shapes and marks, like circles, dashes, and lines. Let it dry for three to five days. The longer it sits, allowing the soy milk to cure, the darker the colour will appear after dyeing.

Dye the Fabric

1. Place about ten avocado pits in a large pot with about 5 quarts + 1 cup (5 litres) of water and let it simmer for two to three hours to create the dye bath. You should see colour start to tint the water.

2. Remove the pits and any other plant debris from the bath. Briefly soak the painted fabric in plain water, and then gently rinse. This will help the fabric take the colour evenly.

3. Place the fabric into the dye bath and simmer at a low boil for two to three more hours, stirring every fifteen to twenty minutes. Make sure the fabric is always completely submerged.

4. Turn off the heat and let the fabric continue to soak overnight. This will make the colour stronger. Keep in mind that the colour will look darkest while the fabric is wet, and it will lighten as it dries.

TIP: SAVE COLOUR
You can save the avocado dye bath and use it again if you'd like, but note that the colour will be weaker after each use.

5. The next day, take the fabric out of the dye bath, squeezing out any excess liquid, and then hang it to dry. Notice that the soy milk design is noticeably darker than the background.

Stitch the Fabric

1. Iron the dyed fabric flat. Lay the backing fabric flat and place the cotton batting on top. Lay the dyed fabric on top of both pieces, and line up all the edges. Use masking tape to hold down the layers; then use safety pins to secure all the layers together. For more detail, see Quilting/Topstitching (page 34).

2. Thread the needle with the perle cotton thread. Begin outlining the soy milk shapes with a running stitch (see Stitch Directory, page 20). Stitch through all three layers. Continue until all the shapes are outlined.

3. Add additional stitched details to some of the shapes for texture. Use any stitches that work with your design. I used seed stitches and linear running stitches to fill a few shapes. Avoid overworking the piece or adding too many stitches to shapes that are near each other. You want the eye to wander and move around.

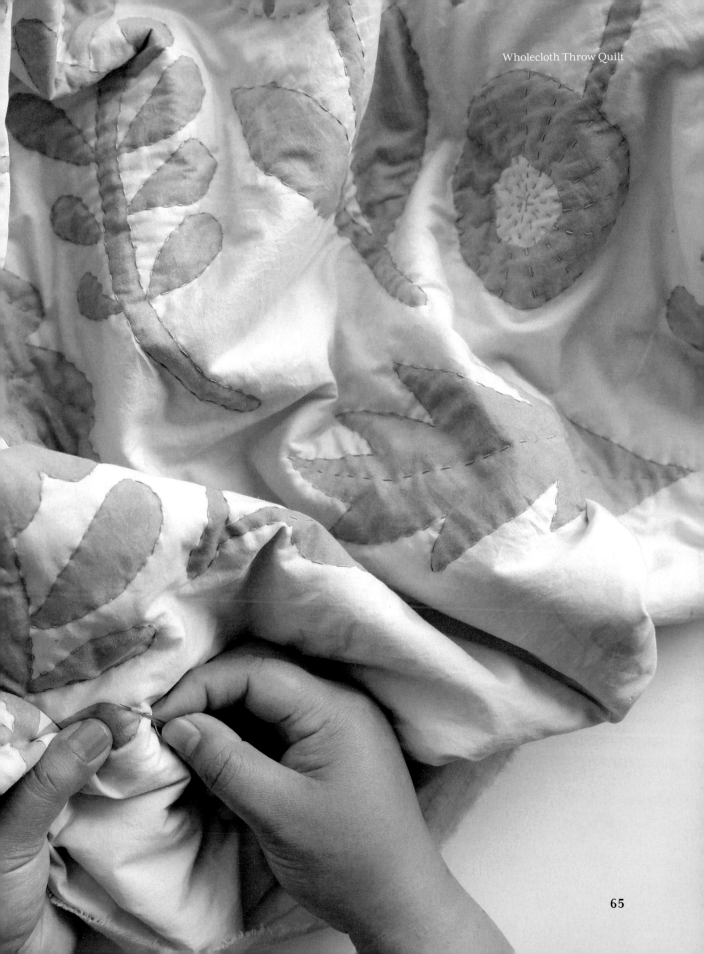

Finish the Quilt

1. Finish the quilt with a self-binding (see Self-Binding: Folding One Layer, page 24). For this project, I put the rolled hem on the back side of the quilt by folding the front layer. Cut the back fabric and batting layers down by about 2.5cm (1″) on each side. Then, working on small areas at a time, roll the raw edge of the top fabric back, with the first fold as close to the cut edge of the other two layers as possible. Then fold one more time onto the back. Secure with a blind stitch (see Stitch Directory, page 20).

2. Add a decorative running stitch around the edge to create a border for the throw, if desired.

Woven Pillow

FINISHED PILLOW: 45.72 × 45.72cm (18″ × 18″)

This pillow project uses hand-block-printed fabric to create strips that are woven together. The weaving process gives the printed shapes the feel of random marks, while the raw edges of the strips suggest an organic and natural quality.

FABRIC

Robert Kaufman Essex Linen

Natural (E014-1242) 1 piece
48.3 × 48.3cm (19″ × 19″)

Lingerie (E064-843) 1 piece
48.3 × 25.4cm (19″ × 10″)

Oyster (E064-1268) 1 piece
48.3 × 25.4cm (19″ × 10″)

Pillow backing 48.3 × 48.3cm
(19″ × 19″)

PRINTING MATERIALS

Soft linoleum (softoleum) or white potatoes to cut out simple shapes

Textile printing ink

Carving tool, size 3 nib

Foam roller

Foam core sheet approximately
50 × 60cm (19¾″ × 23⅝″) as a weaving surface

ADDITIONAL MATERIALS

1 square of iron-on interfacing
48.3 × 48.3cm (19″ × 19″)

1 coordinating zipper 40.6cm (16″) in length

Pillow insert 45.72 × 45.72cm
(18″ × 18″)

Water-soluble marker

Masking tape

Craft knife

Small appliqué pins

Natural colour sewing thread
(Gutermann colour 22 eggshell)

Scissors

Sewing machine with a zipper foot

Serger (optional)

Pinking shears (optional)

Wefty weaving tool

Plate, palette, or ink tray

Notes on Materials

If you don't want to use a zipper, you can do an envelope back closure, which consists of a back made of two pieces of fabric, both with a rolled hem and both measuring a little more than half the size of the pillow. They are sewn in place so that the hemmed edges overlap each other, leaving an unsewn opening. A pillow insert can be placed through this opening. It just requires a bit more fabric because of the overlap.

I am using Speedball brand for both the ink and the carving tool. Printing your own fabric to weave is definitely a fun part of this project, but if you don't have access to the printing materials, you can easily use any printed or patterned fabric that you have on hand. Similarly, feel free to use different fabric. The results will be equally impressive.

Print the Fabric

See Block Printing (page 36) for more information.

1. Carve the linoleum or potatoes to your desired shapes (see Carving a Block, page 38). I used very simple geometric shapes like circles, rings, and half-circles roughly 2.5 to 5cm (1″ to 2″) in size. Keep the shapes simple, because some of the shapes will get torn or covered during the weaving process. To cut the shapes, use a craft knife, like an X-ACTO, and the carving tool with a cutting mat underneath.

If you're carving potatoes, use a cutting board underneath.

2. Wash and dry all the linen for the project; this will help the ink better adhere to the fabric.

3. Spread a little printing ink on a tray, and roll it flat and even using the foam roller. Place the 48.3 × 48.3cm (19″ × 19″) piece of linen on a work surface, and use masking tape to secure it.

4. Roll a thin layer of ink onto the block shapes, and then press them firmly onto the fabric using your fingertips. Gently lift up the shape to reveal the print. If the printed area is faint, you didn't apply enough ink. If it is blotchy, you applied too much ink. It's a good idea to test on a piece of scrap fabric before printing on your good fabric.

5. Repeat the printing process, using all your shapes until the whole surface of the fabric is covered. Make sure to alternate the shapes and to apply ink every time you make a print. Try to create a random arrangement of shapes with an equal amount of unprinted fabric left between each shape.

6. Let the ink fully dry. Then press with an iron on the dry heat setting (no steam) for a few minutes. Iron both the front and back of the printed fabric.

Weave the Fabric

1. Fold the printed fabric in half so that the good sides are facing each other. Then use a ruler and pencil to mark 2.5cm (1″) increments along the entire length of the fold. Take a pair of scissors and snip through the fold of the fabric at each mark about 1.2cm (½″).

2. Starting at each snip, rip the fabric into long strips that are 2.5cm (1″) wide. If you are having difficulty ripping the strips, make the snip a bit bigger.

3. Repeat Steps 1–2 with the two smaller, blank pieces of linen, folding the long side in half and snipping along the fold.

4. Remove any loose threads. Some of the strips might be a bit curly; if needed, give them a quick iron or run them over the sharp edge of a table. You now have two piles of strips for weaving: the printed ones (which will be the warp) and the non printed ones (which will be the weft).

5. Pin the printed strips horizontally onto the foam core, pulling them taut and securing them with pins on both ends. Make each strip parallel to the one next to it, with no space in between and with the ends aligned. This is the warp. Try to be random when placing the strips so as not to mimic the original layout of the fabric print.

6. Start weaving with the non printed strips, beginning in the centre. Use the Wefty tool to hold one of the strips and weave under and over the printed fabric strips. Once you get to the end, make sure the strip is straight, and then secure it by placing a pin on either end of the strip.

7. Continue weaving, alternating between the two colours of non printed strips until the whole surface is woven. Remembering to alternate whether the weave starts over/under or under/over. Use your fingers to adjust each strip so that the strips sit right next to each other.

TIP: WEAVING ALTERNATIVES
If you don't have a Wefty tool, you can try weaving with just your fingertips. Alternatively, cut a cereal box into a strip 2.5 × 10.2cm (1″ × 4″) and tape the fabric to it.

Iron on the Interfacing

1. Before removing the pins from the foam core, place masking tape along the entire outside edge on all four sides of the woven area. This will temporarily secure the edges and keep all the strips in place. Remove all the pins.

2. Turn the weave over, so the good side is facing down. Lay the interfacing on top with the glue side facing the back side of the weaving. Iron the interfacing to the back of the weave and remove the masking tape. Trim to 48.3 × 48.3cm (19″ × 19″) and to neaten the edge if necessary.

Sew the Pillow

1. Serge around all four sides of both the front and back pillow panels. If you don't have a serger, use a zigzag stitch or pinking shears to secure the edges.

2. Place the back panel on top of the front panel with the good sides facing each other. Sew the right edges together with a seam allowance of 1cm (⅜″), leaving a 36.2cm (14¼″) gap in the centre of the seam for the zipper. There should be about 6cm (2⅜″) sewn on either side of the gap. Fold the seam allowance open and iron it flat, including over the unsewn gap. *fig A*

3. Open the pillow and, with the good sides facing up, place the zipper underneath the fabric in the gap. Pin the zipper in place. Using a zipper foot, sew the zipper in place by sewing along both sides and ends of the zipper. *fig B*

4. Open the zipper and fold the pillow so that the good sides are again facing each other. Align all edges. Sew the three remaining sides together using a 1cm (⅜″) seam allowance. *fig C*

5. Turn the pillow right side out. Insert the pillow insert.

A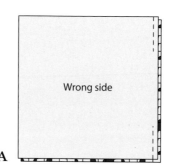

B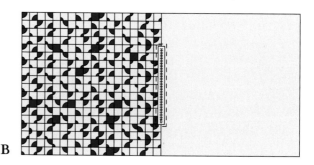

C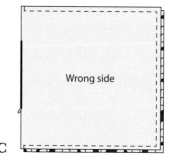

Grid Zipper Pouch

FINISHED POUCH: 20 × 28cm (7⅞″ × 11″)

I've made more than my fair share of pouches with all sorts of surface designs. For this pouch, the front panel is a pattern pieced together using repeated squares of natural linen bordered by smaller rectangles and squares. It's a bold, graphic design that at first seems quite structured, yet the play of colour belies its simplicity and makes this a visually lively pouch.

FABRIC

Remnant cotton or linen in various colours totalling 23 × 30cm (9″ × 11⅞″) when pieced

Cotton or linen fabric for the back of the pouch 23 × 30cm (9″ × 11⅞″)

2 pieces of muslin fabric 23 × 30cm (9″ × 11⅞″) for the lining of the pouch

ADDITIONAL MATERIALS

Water-soluble marker

Paper card (for templates)

Sewing machine and matching thread

Zipper foot

Fabric scissors

Paper scissors

Metal or plastic zipper 26cm (10¼″)

Leather cord and wood toggle
(or zipper pull of your choice)

CUTTING

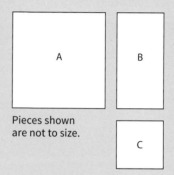

Pieces shown are not to size.

There are three shapes needed to piece this design. Create templates from the paper card using the dimensions listed, then cut:

- 12 A squares 8 × 8cm (3¼″ × 3¼″)
- 17 B rectangles 3.5 × 8cm (1⅜″ × 3¼″)
- 6 C squares 3.5 × 3.5cm (1⅜″ × 1⅜″)

Notes on Materials

The grid pattern for this pouch design has so many possibilities with colour placement, so feel free to make any colour combinations you like. You can also make many different variations based on this one design.

Stitch the Patchwork

1. Create blocks for the pouch by sewing shape A and shape B together using a 1cm (⅜″) seam allowance. Sew a separate shape B and shape C together. Then sew these two pieces together to create what appears to be a square bordered with an L shape. Repeat six times to create six separate blocks.

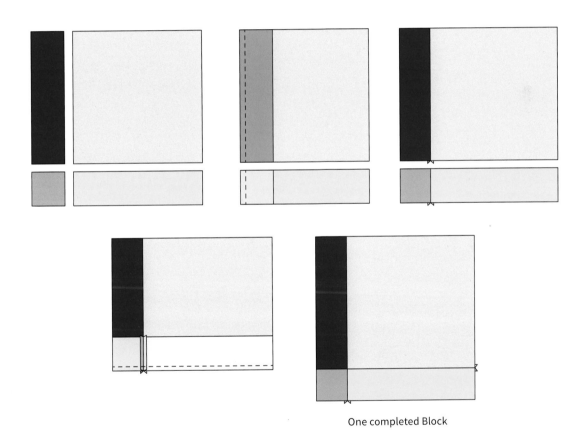

One completed Block

2. Sew all six blocks together to create two attached rows of three blocks.

3. To finish the rest of the front panel, sew a shape B to the bottom of a shape A with a 1cm (⅜") seam allowance. Repeat this one more time with the same unit so that you have a vertical row of A/B/A/B from top to bottom. Then sew this to the left short side of the panel. Next, similarly, sew a horizontal row consisting of shapes A/B/A/B/A/B/A. Sew this to the bottom of the main front panel as shown in Diagram A. The completed panel should be 23 × 30cm (9" × 11⅞"), which includes a 1cm (⅜") seam allowance around the entire outside edge.

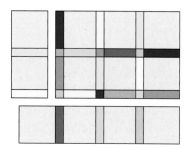

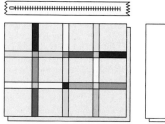

Diagram A: All pieces ready for sewing

Sew the Pouch

1. Lay the front panel good side up. Place the zipper along the top of one long side, edges aligned, centred, and facing down. Place the lining on top of the zipper, good side facing down, also aligned along the top of the front panel. Using a zipper foot, sew the front panel, the zipper, and the lining together along the top edge with a 1cm (⅜″) seam allowance. Turn the lining and front panel over to expose the zipper. The zipper is still facing down. *fig A*

2. To attach the other side, lay the back side of the pouch, good side facing up, underneath the zipper aligned along the unsewn edge. Place the second lining on top of the zipper also aligned along the unsewn zipper edge, good side down. Sew along the zipper edge with a 1cm (⅜″) seam allowance. Fold open so that both linings are on top and the front and back are below with their good sides facing down. *fig B*

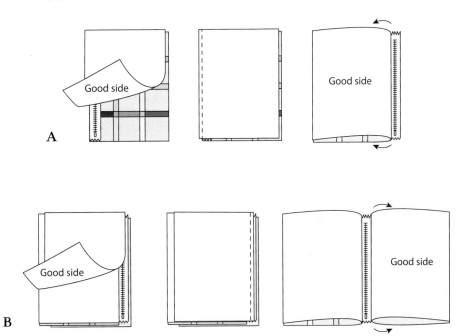

A

B

3. Fold the pouch so that the linings are together, good sides facing each other, and the front and back are together, good sides facing each other. Sew around the outside edge of all four sides, leaving an unsewn opening on one side of the lining about 10cm (4″) wide so that you can turn the pouch right side out. Sew gussets 5cm (2″) wide on all four corners. *fig C*

4. Turn the pouch right side out by pulling the outside of the pouch through the unsewn gap in the lining. Finally, sew the opening in the lining closed using your sewing machine and place the lining inside the pouch. *fig D*

5. If you are using a leather cord and wood toggle (or bead), fold the cord in half, feed the loose ends through the toggle, and tie the two ends together to form a knot. Then feed the loop end of the cord through the zipper pull and feed the toggle through the loop to make a knot. As an alternative, you can use a ribbon or cord of your choice.

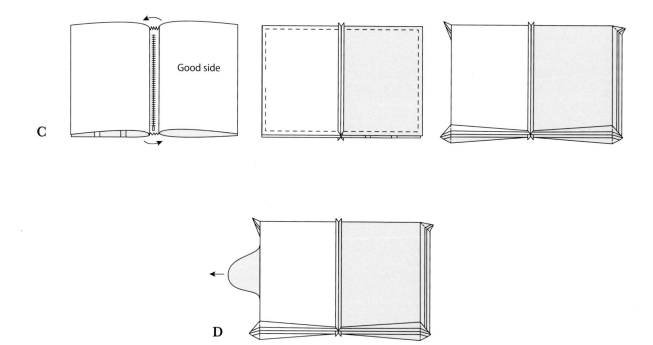

Good side

C

D

Tool Roll

FINISHED TOOL ROLL: 18 × 19cm (7″ × 7½″)

Quilting on a small scale is a perfect way to make useful everyday items like a tool roll—a place to store and protect your craft tools, brushes, or pens and pencils. I use tool rolls in my studio and when I travel. For this one, I wanted to try a simple sun-printing technique by creating a resist surface design with found objects. This design can be any colour you like, uses easily found ingredients, and is really fast.

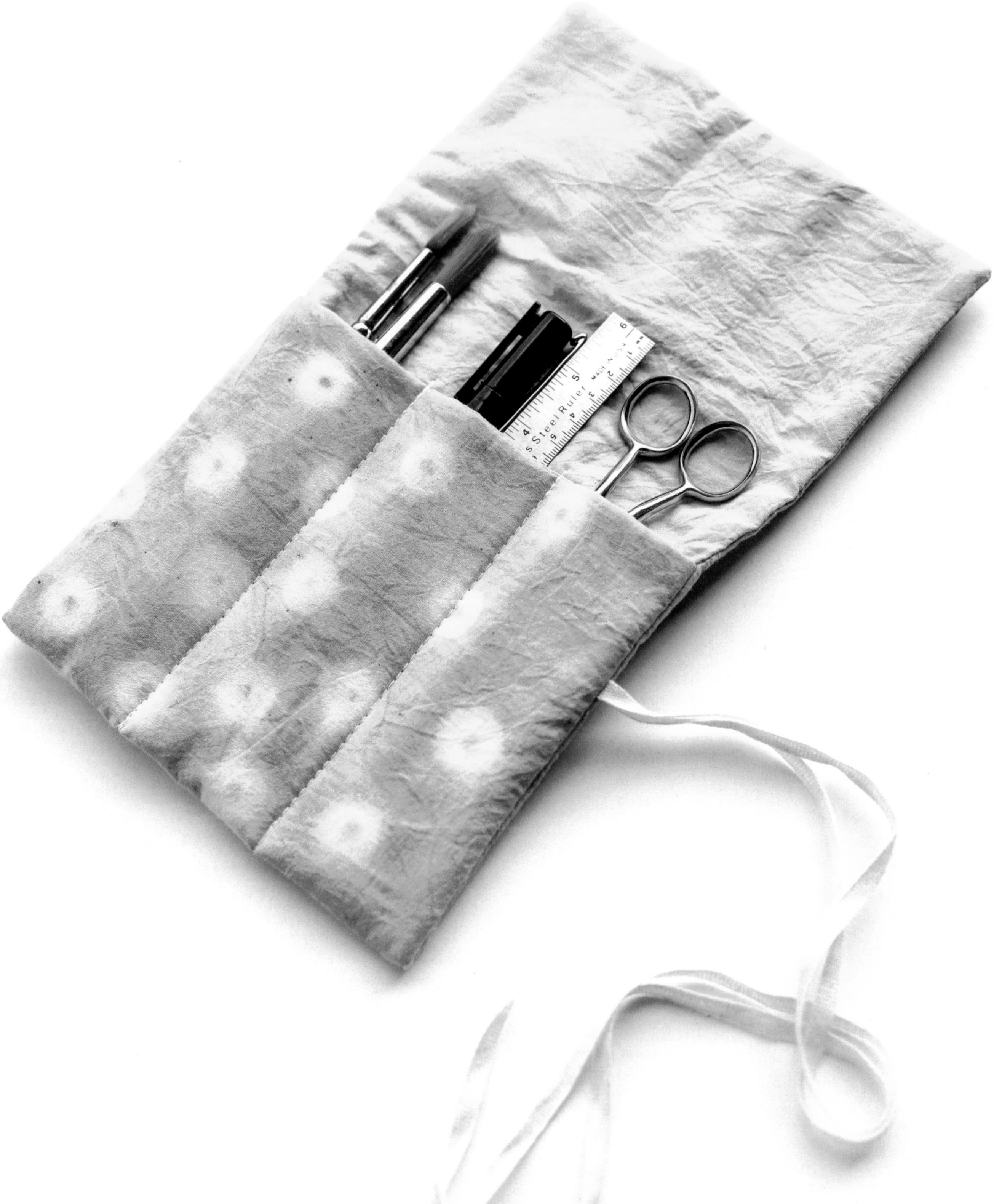
Steel Ruler

FABRIC

Cotton fabric rectangle 20 × 47cm (7⅞″ × 18½″)

Fabric rectangle 20 × 47cm (7⅞″ × 18½″) for the lining of the roll

Low-loft cotton batting 20 × 47cm (7⅞″ × 18½″)

ADDITIONAL MATERIALS

Plastic drop cloth

Masking tape

Safety pins or small appliqué pins

Sewing machine

Thread

Fabric scissors

Hand-sewing needle

DYE MATERIALS

Iron

½ cup (125mL) soy milk

1 teaspoon (5mL) yellow procion dye mix or any colour you would like to use

1 cup (250mL) metal washers

Wide flat brush 10cm (4″) wide or wider

100cm (40″) narrow twine

1 cup (250mL) soda ash

Mixing container

Notes on Materials

As an option, you can add topstitching around the dyed shapes to give the pouch more texture. You can also try different resist objects on the fabric to experiment with a variety of shapes. You need to dye the fabric in direct sunlight, so make sure to have an area prepared and to dye at the right time of day.

Create the Fabric Design

1. Create a bath for preparing the fabric by mixing a ratio of 1 cup (250mL) of soda ash into 1 gallon (4.5L) of water. Soak the cotton fabric in the mixture for 20 minutes; then lay flat to dry. Leave the lining natural for a nice contrast, or dye it following the same Steps 1–4, if you like.

2. Lay the dried fabric on top of a small plastic drop cloth. In a small container, mix the soy milk and procion dye (cold water dye). Using the brush, apply the soy/dye mixture over the entire surface of the fabric until it's wet.

3. Keeping the fabric on the plastic to prevent the dye from staining any table surface, move the fabric into a spot with direct sunlight. Place the washers (or other found objects) over the entire surface of the wet fabric in whatever pattern you like. I spaced them randomly. Let the fabric sit in the sun until it is completely dry. Remove the objects. The washers work by blocking the sun, resulting in a pattern of lighter yellow circles.

4. Leave the fabric to set for a couple of days; then gently rinse it in warm soapy water for a few minutes. Let it dry and iron it flat.

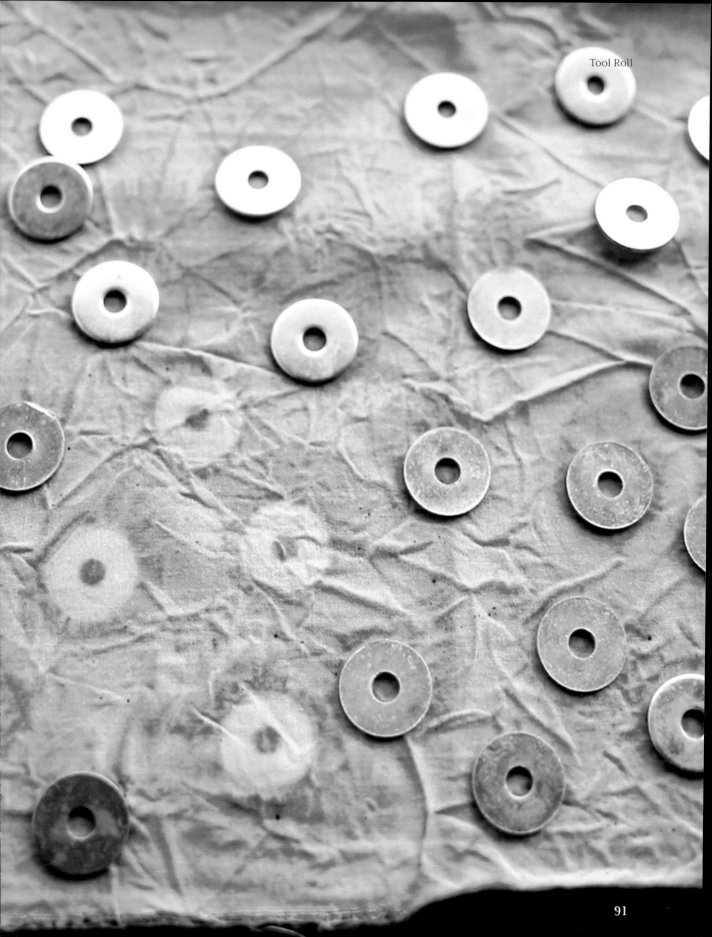

Sew the Tool Roll

1. Place the dyed fabric on top of the lining so that the good sides are facing each other. Then place both pieces on top of the batting. Align all edges neatly. *fig A*

2. Stitch along one of the short ends, through all three layers, with a 1cm (⅜″) seam allowance. *fig B*

3. Fold the sewn edge up so that it is about half the length of the fabric stack, about 15cm (6″) from the top as shown. While keeping the fold in place, pull the dyed fabric layer out and back so that it is facing up. *fig C*

4. Cut approximately 100cm (40″) of narrow twine or ribbon. Fold in half. Lay the ribbon on top of the printed fabric about 5cm (2″) below the seam, with the folded end extending out about 2.5cm (1″) beyond the edge of the printed fabric. *fig D*

5. Keeping the fold in place, fold the remaining portion of the dyed fabric back over the sewn edge and lay flat. You may have to adjust the folds slightly so that both the folds at the bottom are aligned and the unsewn edges at the top are also aligned. *fig E*

6. Sew all the layers together along the three remaining raw edges, the sides and top, with a 1cm (⅜″) seam allowance, leaving a small gap, about 10cm (4″) along the top, unfolded side. *fig F*

7. Pull the tool roll right side out through the unsewn gap and flatten with your fingers to create nice corners. *fig G*

8. Hand sew the gap closed with a blind stitch (see Stitch Directory, page 20). Press the tool roll with an iron.

9. Using the sewing machine, stitch over the pocket area to create divided tool slots. I stitched the pocket into three sections, but add more or fewer based on your desired use. *fig H*

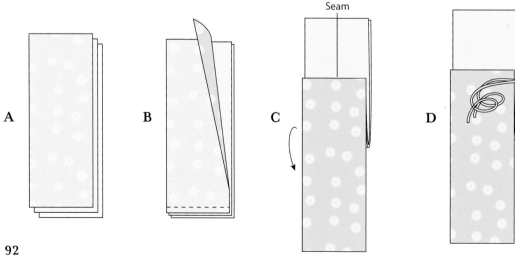

A   B   C   D

Seam

E

F

G

H

Square Drawstring Bag

FINISHED BAG: 20 × 20 × 20cm (7⅞″ × 7⅞″ × 7⅞″)

This drawstring bag is inspired by Japanese rice bags called Komebukuros. It's very simple to sew up and consists of five equal squares. The four sides are half log cabin patchworks made from indigo dyed fabric. It can be easily modified to be smaller or larger. Because the flat bottom helps it stand up and the added batting gives it a nice structure, I think it's a perfect project bag.

FABRIC

⅛ yard (11.4cm) pieces each of 8 assorted colours

Solid piece of fabric 22 × 22cm (8⅝″ × 8⅝″) for the bottom panel

½ yard (45.7cm) of muslin for lining

½ yard (45.7cm) of low-loft cotton batting

Strip of fabric 2.5 × 70cm (1″ × 27⅝″) for the loops

Strip of fabric 2.5 × 96cm (1″ × 37¾″) or 1 yard of cotton rope for the drawstring

ADDITIONAL MATERIALS

Water-soluble marker

Paper card to make templates

Masking tape

Safety pins or small appliqué pins

Fabric scissors

Paper scissors

Sewing machine

Thread

Ruler

Iron

Bias tape maker (optional)

CUTTING

Muslin Lining: Cut 5 squares 22 × 22cm (8⅝″ × 8⅝″).

Cotton Batting: Cut 5 squares 22 × 22cm (8⅝″ × 8⅝″).

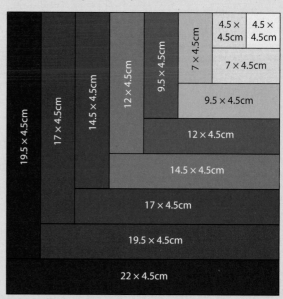

Cutting diagram. Sizes include seam allowances. I suggest using metric measurements when cutting this block for best precision and accuracy.

Notes on Materials

This project is a good way to play with colour, and since there are four sides, you can treat each panel differently if you wish. This pattern includes batting to give it a softer structure, but feel free to exclude it or replace it with interfacing for added stiffness.

When gathering fabric to patch the sides of the bag, keep in mind that you will need to have enough fabric for the patchwork seam allowance. The drawstring in my project is made of the same fabric as the bag, but if you have a nice cord or leather piece, either would make a nice substitute.

Patch the Fabric

In my log cabin blocks, I used indigo dyed fabric. I used darker shades for the larger strips and then progressively lighter ones for the middle and corner pieces. The structure for each side is the same, but I rotated each panel 180°, so each side appears a little different. There is plenty of room for experimentation—you can create an ombre of similar colours or use completely different colours or prints arranged from dark to light. Refer to the cutting diagram for specific measurements.

1. Each block consists of strips 4.5cm (1¾″) wide. With a 1cm (⅜″) seam allowance, each strip in the finished block will be 2.5cm (1″). Refer to the cutting diagram for lengths and colours.

Each piece in the diagram is sized for cutting and is labelled with an alphabetical letter to signify the order in which they are sewn together. I tend to cut longer strips than I need and then cut them to size while sewing. Using a clear quilter's ruler makes it very easy to cut repeated widths and lengths. You can also use paper card to make templates if you prefer. Cut out shapes A–O for all four blocks.

2. Sew the pieces together with a 1cm (⅜″) seam allowance. Start in the corner by attaching A to B. Sew C to the long side, trim, and then sew D to the left side. Work progressively, sewing each piece in alphabetical order, from row to row, trimming as you proceed. Make sure to keep the edges and the whole block nice and square.

3. Repeat to piece three more blocks. These are the sides of the bag.

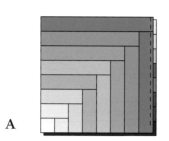

A

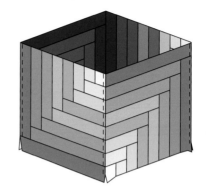

Sew the Bag

1. With the sides of the bag arranged as you wish, align two panels, good sides together, and sew along one side with a 1cm (⅜″) seam allowance, leaving about 1cm (⅜″) at the bottom of each seam unsewn. This makes it easier to attach the bottom panel later on. Repeat to attach all four side panels. The sides should now form a square box with good sides facing in. *fig A*

2. Pin the bottom panel to the bottoms of all four side panels, good side facing in, and sew all the way around with a 1cm (⅜″) seam allowance. The unsewn space you left at the bottom of the sides will help with sewing the bottom in place. Trim the tips of the corners so that when you turn it right side out, it won't be bulky. Turn it right side out. *fig B*

3. Lay one piece of batting onto the wrong side of each lining piece. Sew together on all edges. Trim any extra batting so that all edges are aligned and neat.

4. Repeat Steps 1–2 for the lining/batting panels, sewing the four pieces together to form a square box with the batting facing out. Leave a 10cm (4″) gap in the centre of one of the corner seams. Attach the bottom panel and trim the corners. Keep the good sides facing in. *fig C*

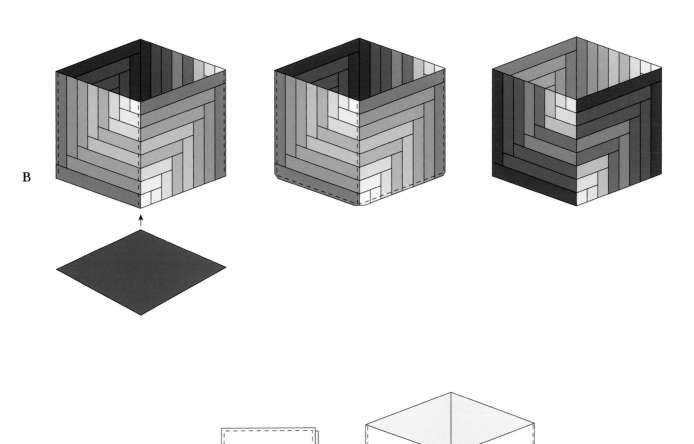

B

C

Batting

Sew the Loops

1. Fold the strip of fabric for the loops lengthwise so both raw edges meet in the middle, good side out. Iron. Fold again, in half. Iron again. If you have a bias tape maker, you can use it to fold and iron the strip.

2. Sew the strip closed, along the entire length, keeping close to the edge. Then cut the long strip into eight smaller strips, each around 8cm (3⅛″) long. This length already includes seam allowances. Fold each strip in half. *fig A*

3. Sew the loops to the patchwork half of the bag along the top edge. Place the loops upside down on each corner seam and in the centre of each panel. Sew each loop with a 1cm (⅜″) seam allowance on the loop itself, but with a scant seam allowance on the bag. *fig B*

4. Place the patchwork portion of the bag and the loops inside the lining portion of the bag so that the good sides are facing each other. The batting should be facing out. Sew all around the top edge of the bag with a 1cm (⅜″) seam allowance. *fig C*

5. Turn the good sides out through the unsewn gap in the lining. Hand sew the gap closed with a blind stitch (see Stitch Directory, page 20). Topstitch using a sewing machine along the top of the edge of the bag so that the loops are standing straight up.

6. If you are using a cotton rope, thread it through the loops. If you are using fabric to make the drawstring, follow Steps 1–2, but do not cut the drawstring into smaller pieces. Tie knots at the ends of the fabric drawstring to prevent fraying, or fold the fabric in and sew the ends closed. Thread the fabric drawstring through the loops and tie the ends together. *fig D*

A

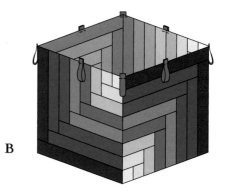

B

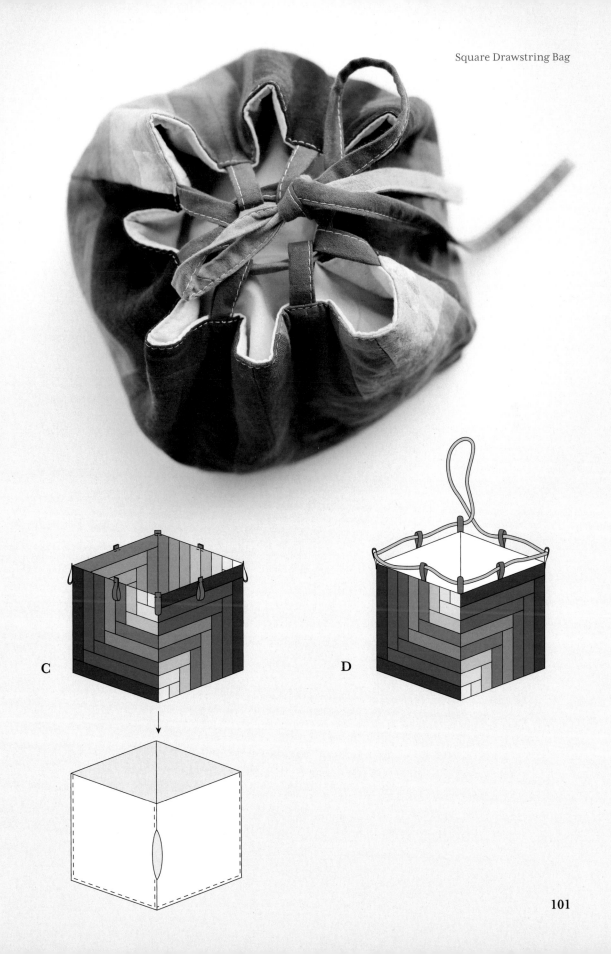

C

D

Mug Rug

FINISHED RUG: 27 × 27cm (10⅝″ × 10⅝″)

A mug rug is a very quick and simple project. It's a quilted mat that is big enough for your coffee and a snack. Of course, it's not that limited! In fact, this project is very versatile and is perfect for a planted pot or for your night stand. Smaller projects like this are also a nice way to use up remnants, even ones with odd shapes, and a great way to experiment with colour and pattern.

FABRIC

One or two pieces of coloured linen that combine to approximately 28 × 28cm (11″ × 11″)

One piece of fabric for the backing approximately 28 × 28cm (11″ × 11″)

Remnant pieces of fabric in various colours

Low-loft cotton batting approximately 28 × 28cm (11″ × 11″)

ADDITIONAL MATERIALS

Ruler

Hera marker

Water-soluble pencil (optional)

Safety pins and straight pins

Hand-sewing needle

Sewing machine and thread

Topstitching or quilting thread in a contrasting colour (I used WonderFil perle cotton colour SP101)

Iron

PATTERN (OPTIONAL)

If you would like to appliqué the same shapes that I use, refer to the freeform shapes in this illustration.

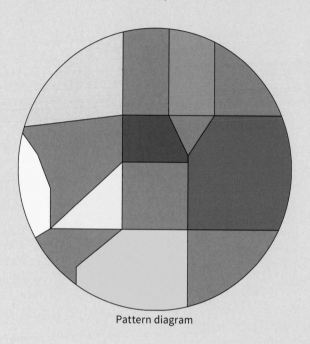

Pattern diagram

Appliqué the Top

1. Create the base cloth using one or two pieces of fabric. I sewed two pieces of grey linen together that are very close in colour with a 1cm (⅜″) seam allowance. The finished base cloth should be about 28 × 28cm (11″ × 11″). Press the seam and fold the piece into quarters.

2. Using a water-soluble pencil, draw round corners so that the piece is not perfectly square or circular but has a nice organic shape. Trim along the lines.

3. Cut the coloured remnant fabrics into several random shapes. Refer to the pattern diagram if you'd like to use the same shapes I used. Keep in mind that you don't want to completely cover the base cloth fabric. Lay down each piece of scrap on the base fabric, paying attention to the negative space.

4. When you have found your desired arrangement, appliqué the shapes to the fabric. Turn the edges of the appliqué shapes under as you sew a blind stitch along the folded edge with a 1cm (⅜″) seam allowance (see Needle-Turn Appliqué, page 32). The edges of the appliqués that will be caught in the seam allowance do not need to be sewn down.

Sewing Together

1. Cut the backing fabric and batting to match the same shape as the front fabric. Lay the backing fabric on top of the front piece with good sides facing each other. Place the batting on top of the backing. Pin the layers together and sew around the edge using a 1cm (⅜″) seam allowance. Leave an unsewn opening around 10cm (4″) anywhere around the edge of the rug. *fig A*

2. Cut small darts (triangles) into the seam allowance around the entire edge of the piece so that when you turn it right side out, the edge will have a nice curve. See Self Binding: Sewn Edge (page 25). Turn it right side out through the unsewn gap. Hand sew the gap closed with a blind stitch (see Stitch Directory, page 20). *fig B*

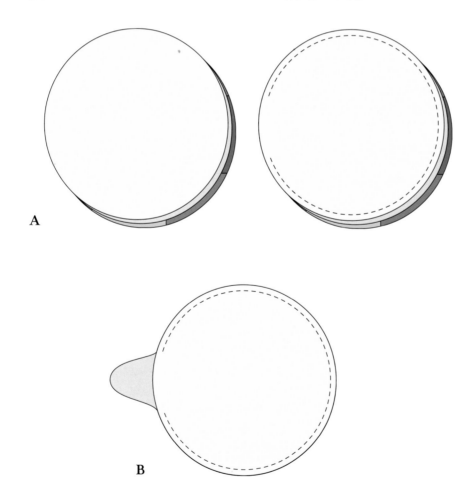

A

B

C

3. With a ruler and Hera marker, make a series of perpendicular creases, approximately 2cm (¾″) wide, across the entire piece. Use the needle and contrasting colour thread to sew a running stitch along the creased lines, making sure to sew through all three layers. *figs C–E*

4. Optional: Add a small fabric loop on one side so that you can hang the rug on the wall when you're not using it. Make the loop from a piece of twill tape about 1.2cm (½″) wide and 15.2cm (6″) long. This can be placed on the inside before sewing the piece closed, or you can sew it on the outside using a whipstitch.

D

E

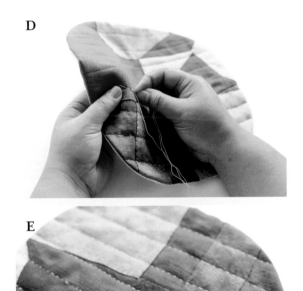

Cross-Body Bag

FINISHED BAG: 38 × 29 × 20cm (15″ × 11½″ × 7⅞″)
STRAP: 105cm (41⅜″) long

Quilting is perfect for wearable items. Quilted items have a softness to them that makes them really comfortable. The quilted body of this bag also gives it a nice shape, but with a loose structure that keeps it casual. It has a bucket bottom and some interior pockets, so it has lots of room for all of your essentials during everyday outings.

FABRIC

Exterior

Cotton or linen ¼ yard (22.9cm) each of two colours, equal to a panel 39.5 × 31cm (15½″ × 12¼″)

Cotton or linen 39.5 × 31cm (15½″ × 12¼″) for back panel

Cotton or linen oval 21 × 28.5cm (8¼″ × 11¼″), matching one of the colours on the outside of the bag

Lining (lightweight canvas or muslin)

Two pieces 39.5 × 31cm (15½″ × 12¼″)

One oval 21 × 28.5cm (8¼″ × 11¼″)

One piece 26 × 20cm (10¼″ × 7⅞″) for the interior pocket (optional)

Strap

Cotton or linen 16 × 107cm (6¼″ × 42⅛″), matching one of the colours on the outside of the bag

BATTING

Strip for the strap 16 × 107cm (6¼″ × 42⅛″)

Two pieces 39.5 × 31cm (15½″ × 12¼″)

One oval 21 × 28.5cm (8¼″ × 11¼″)

ADDITIONAL MATERIALS

Safety pins or small appliqué pins

Sewing machine and thread

Fabric scissors

Hera marker

Hand-sewing needle

Topstitching or quilting thread in a coordinating colour

Iron

Notes on Materials

For the outside fabric, I used two shades of cotton that I dyed with indigo. You can dye your own fabric or purchase any solid or printed fabric. The cotton is lightweight on its own, but in combination with the batting and lining, the bag has a nice overall weight and structure. If you want the strap to be longer or shorter, adjust the length of the fabric strip. You can omit the strap batting if you'd like, but it offers nice comfort.

Sew the Patchwork

The patchwork for this bag doesn't have a specific pattern—it's all done free-form and improvisationally, but with a limited palette of only two colours. For more on sewing patchwork, see Putting Things Together (page 26).

To form the pattern shown, cut a series of strips in different widths from both colours. Arrange them randomly; then sew them together in groups of two, three, or four along their long sides. Cut the groups into various sizes of squares and rectangles; then piece the squares and rectangles together so that the strips run parallel to each other. Form a panel 39.5 × 31cm (15½″ × 12¼″). Piece the panel with a 1cm (⅜″) seam allowance. Press.

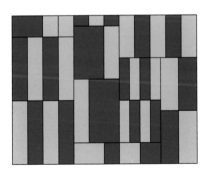

Sew the Bag

1. Place the back panel on top of the front patchwork panel with the good sides facing each other. Place one rectangle of batting on top of the two panels and one rectangle of batting below the two panels. Pin all four layers together with the edges aligned. Sew along the two short sides with a 1cm (⅜″) seam allowance, leaving the top and bottom unsewn. *fig A*

2. For the bottom of the bag, place the batting oval on the back of the exterior fabric oval. Sew the two pieces together, as close to the edge as possible. Trim any excess batting. With the good side of the oval panel facing up and the batting facing down, place it inside between the front and back panels, along the bottom of the bag, pinning it to the bottom edge. Sew along the edge with your sewing machine using a 1cm (⅜″) seam allowance. To avoid stretching and puckering, sew with the oval shape flat on the sewing table. Cut notches into the seam allowance around the entire edge, and then turn the bag right side out. *fig B*

3. Create a 1cm (⅜″) rolled hem along one of the long sides of the interior pocket fabric. To do this, simply roll one edge over to the back side about 0.6cm (¼″), and smooth it flat. Then fold it again about 1cm (⅜″) so that the raw edge is hidden. Sew along the edge of the hem through all layers with your sewing machine, or hand stitch with a blind stitch (see Stitch Directory, page 20).

4. With the hem at the top, centre the pocket onto one of the of the lining panels, about 10cm (4″) down from the top edge. Using a sewing machine, sew along the remaining three edges of the pocket, folding the edges under about 1cm (⅜″) as you sew. If you'd like, add an additional topstitch around the three sides of the pocket to add strength. *fig C*

5. Repeat Steps 1–2 to sew the two lining pieces together along the side seams, good sides together. Leave a 10cm (4″) gap in the centre of one of the side seams. Attach to the lining oval. Make sure the pocket is on the inside. Leave the good sides facing in. *fig D*

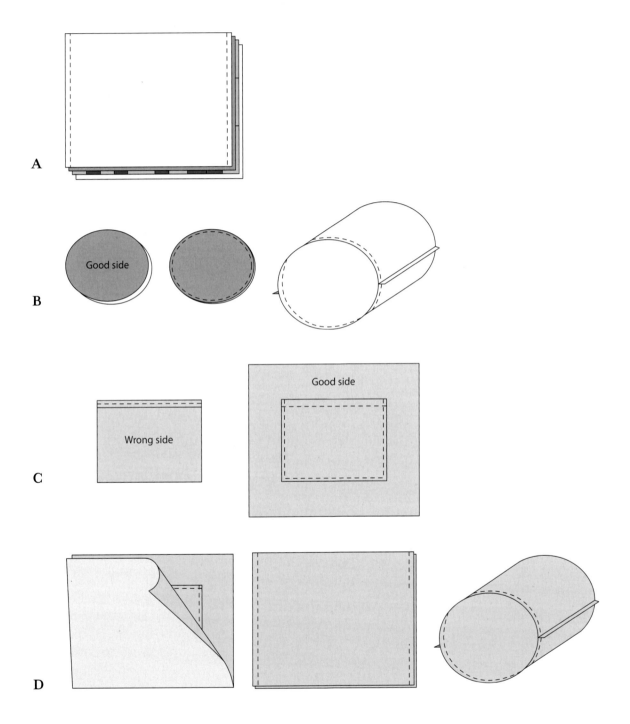

A

B

Good side

C

Wrong side

Good side

D

Make the Strap

1. Without batting: Iron the strap fabric in half lengthwise with the good side facing in, and sew along the edge with a 1cm (⅜″) seam allowance. Turn right side out, and press so that the seam is in the middle. Sew two lines of topstitching along both edges the entire length.

2. With batting: Lay the strap fabric good side facing up, on top of the strap batting, with all edges aligned. Next, fold the batting and fabric together in half lengthwise with the batting on the outside. Pin the fold together if necessary. Then sew all layers together along the unfolded edge. Leave the ends open. Turn the strap right side out. Then, as above, press the strap so that the sewn seam is in the middle. Topstitch along the entire length. I made three lines of stitching, equally spaced.

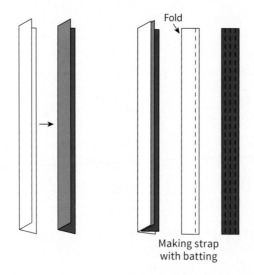

Making strap
with batting

Finish the Bag

1. Place the ends of the strap along the top edge of the outer part of the bag with the good sides facing each other. Make sure to place the strap centred along the seams of the bag and with the ends pointing up. You can pin to hold in place, or sew in place close to the top edge of the bag.

2. Place the outer part of the bag and strap inside the lining with the good sides facing each other and the top edges aligned. Make sure the interior pocket is on the opposite side from the patchwork. Sew all around the top edge of the bag with a 1cm (⅜″) seam allowance. Turn the bag right side out by pulling it through the unsewn gap in the lining. Hand sew the gap closed with a whipstitch (see Stitch Directory, page 20). Sew a topstitch close to the edge around the entire top edge through all layers and the strap.

3. To add topstitching through all three layers of the front patchwork panel, work on a table or the end of an ironing board so that the front panel is laying flat. Crease a series of vertical parallel lines using a Hera marker, spaced about 5cm (2″) apart. Hand stitch a running stitch along all crease lines.

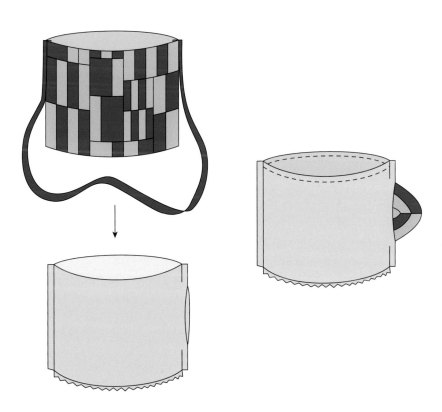

Appliqué Wallet

FINISHED WALLET: 14 × 20cm (5½″ × 7⅞″) folded

For me, there are a couple of approaches to creating appliqué. The first is to work in a free-form manner, cutting shapes by hand and laying them down on a base cloth until I like what I see. The second is to work from a drawing and create templates that determine the placement of shapes. In this project, there is potential for either approach.

In fact, this is a project with a lot of possibilities. My initial intent was to make a little wallet, but it occurred to me that by adding a felt band on the inside flap for needles and pins that it would also make a great sewing kit. If you'd prefer a little cross-body bag, then all you have to do is add a long strap. And, of course, you can create the appliqué by following the pattern or you can create a design of your own.

FABRIC

Cotton rectangle 20 × 38cm (7⅞″ × 15″)

Cotton muslin rectangle 20 × 38cm (7⅞″ × 15″) for lining

Cotton strip or bias trim 3.8 × 20cm (1½″ × 7⅞″)

Cotton strip or bias trim 3.8 × 72cm (1½″ × 28⅜″)

Low-loft cotton batting 20 × 38cm (7⅞″ × 15″)

Fabric remnants in various colours or textures

Felt scrap 20 × 5cm (7⅞″ × 2″) (optional)

ADDITIONAL MATERIALS

Water-soluble marker

Paper card to make templates

Masking tape

Safety pins or small appliqué pins

Hand-sewing needle

Black sewing thread

Fabric scissors

Iron

Tracing paper

Snap domes or buttons (optional)

Notes on Materials

When you are doing needle-turn appliqué, the shapes will sit flatter if the fabric is not heavy. So, try to choose fabric that is tightly woven and lightweight. A quilting cotton would work well too.

PATTERN (OPTIONAL)

If you would like to appliqué the same shapes that I use, refer to the diagram below. You need to include a 1cm (⅜″) seam allowance on each shape. On the diagram, you will notice there are faded lines which indicate overlapping shapes.

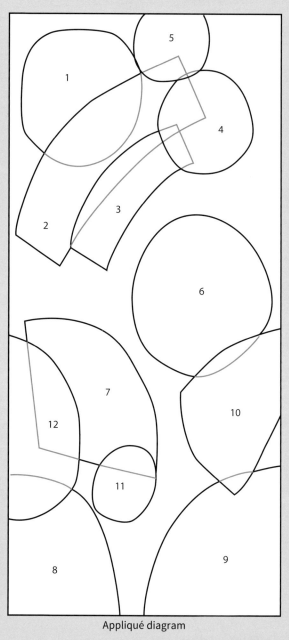

Appliqué diagram

Stitch the Appliqué

See Appliqué (page 32) for more information.

1. Create paper card templates of all the appliqué shapes (see Patching with a Template, page 30). If you're creating templates based on the Appliqué diagram, double the size of the shapes as they appear in this book. Trace the templates onto the fabrics of your choice using a water-soluble marker; then cut them out.

If you're creating your own appliqué shapes, feel free to draw directly onto fabric or make templates based on your own designs. The finished appliqué pieces should fit on the panel 20 × 38cm (7⅞″ × 15″).

2. Place the base fabric good side up. Lay the fabric shapes out onto the base cloth according to the supplied pattern or as desired. Some shapes might extend beyond the edge of the base cloth due to their added seam allowances, and some shapes will overlap others based on the pattern. Appliqué bottom shapes first by starting with number one on the diagram.

3. Appliqué all of the shapes into place (see Needle-Turn Appliqué, page 32). Depending on the fabric you chose, you may find that you have to snip a bit of the fabric in the seam allowance so that curves will be less bulky when you turn the fabric under. I used a blind stitch with a contrasting black thread, which results in small, but still visible stitches. Use a whipstitch if you want the stitching to be even more visible (see Stitch Directory, page 20).

Sew the Wallet

1. Optional: If you want to create a sewing booklet, sew the felt pin holder in place first. Using your sewing machine, sew the felt strip onto the good side of the lining, about 2.5cm (1″) from the top edge. Sew across both long sides of the felt. The short sides will get sewn later when the edge binding is sewn in place.

2. Place the lining face down. Place the batting on top, and then place the appliquéd panel, facing up, on top of the batting. Trim any pieces or extra shapes so that all edges are neat and aligned. If you are making a sewing booklet, make sure that the felt patch on the lining is facing down and is on the opposite end to where you will place the bias trim in the next step.

3. Grab the 20cm (7⅞″) strip for the bias trim on the short side of the wallet. Place the fabric strip on the good side of the appliqué panel, aligning with the top edge and sides. Hold in place with pins. Sew with a 1cm (⅜″) seam allowance along the entire length using a machine or by hand using a backstitch. Then fold it over to the other side of the panel, including over the batting, onto the front of the lining, and pin it in place. Fold the raw edge underneath, and hand sew it down with a blind stitch (see Stitch Directory, page 20) along the entire length. Make sure to pull the fabric down so that it's a snug fit. See Single-Edge Folded Binding (page 22) for more information. *fig A*

4. With the appliqué side facing down and the lining facing up, fold the end of the panel with the bias trim over onto the lining to create a pocket that measures 14cm (5½″) high, with the remaining area a flap measuring 10cm (4″). Using a sewing machine or by hand, sew along the sides, very close to the edge, to sew the pocket in place. *fig B*

5. Using the second, longer piece of bias, repeat Step 2 to create a bias trim edge with the fabric on the remaining three unfinished sides of the wallet (see Complete Folded Binding, page 23). *fig C*

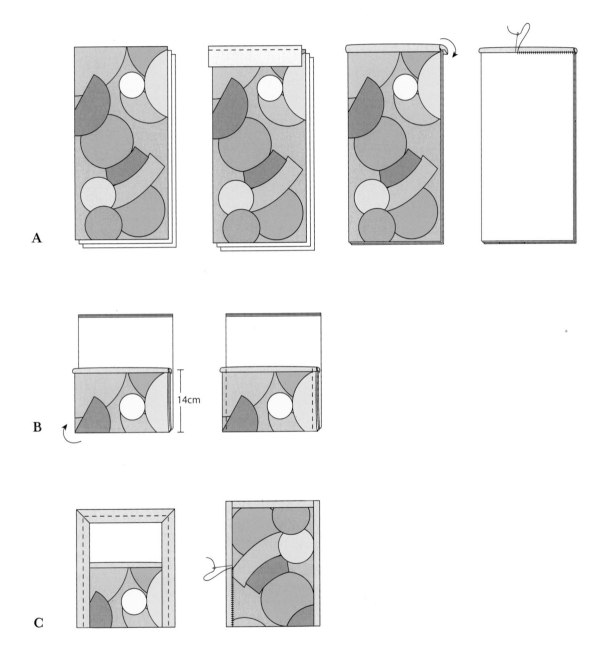

A

B

14cm

C

6. Optional: Sew two snap domes on either side of the inside flap for closure. You can skip this step completely, or instead use a button and a piece of string to secure the flap.

Squeeze-Frame Pouch

FINISHED POUCH: 12.7 × 12.7cm (5″ × 5″)

This handy little squeeze pouch is great to hold coins, small notions, or any little thing that is easily lost. A metal squeeze/flex frame is used for the mouth, while the body consists of a lined patchwork made of small remnants that you have on hand. You can also make the pattern longer and use this as a glasses holder or pencil case.

FABRIC

¼ yard (22.9cm) of scraps and remnants for exterior

¼ yard (22.9cm) of lining

Remnant of lining fabric for top band

ADDITIONAL MATERIALS

Metal squeeze/flex frame 12cm (4¾") wide

Water-soluble marker

Paper card to make templates

Pins

Fabric scissors

Iron

Pliers

CUTTING

The dimensions below include 1cm (⅜") seam allowance.

Cut two exterior top bands: 6.5 × 16.5cm (2½" × 6½")

Cut two lining fabric top bands: 6.5 × 16.5cm (2½" × 6½")

Cut two lining fabric body of pouch: 13.3 × 16.5cm (5¼" × 6½")

Pouch Body Exterior Patchwork

For two patched exteriors (one per side):

Using the dimensions shown in the diagrams, cut:

- Cut eight of each shape A, B, and C

  To make the square A angle, find the center point of 2 adjacent sides and cut from point to point.

- Cut four of each shape D and E

Notes on Materials

The patchwork portion for this project is quite open-ended. While I used remnant linen, you can use any fabric on hand in any colour combination. Remnants of printed fabric can also look great. If you're not following the pattern provided for piecing, create two panels 13.3 × 16.5cm (5¼" × 6½") for the front and back of the pouch.

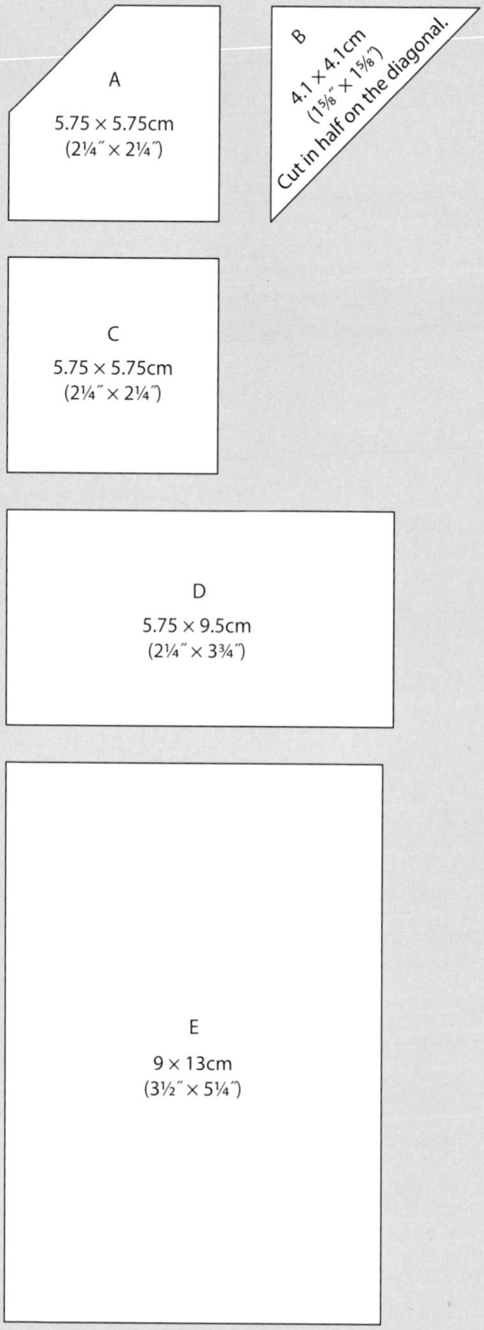

A
5.75 × 5.75cm
(2¼" × 2¼")

B
4.1 × 4.1cm
(1⅝" × 1⅝")
Cut in half on the diagonal.

C
5.75 × 5.75cm
(2¼" × 2¼")

D
5.75 × 9.5cm
(2¼" × 3¾")

E
9 × 13cm
(3½" × 5¼")

Diagrams shown are not to scale.

Cut the Fabric

1. Construct the coloured patchwork panels using the cut pieces and construction diagram. Sew one shape A to one shape B. Then sew the A/B shape to shape C as shown. Repeat. Rotate one of the two groups 180°. Sew the two groups together to make a square. Finish the front panel by sewing the square to shape D and then sewing the entire piece to shape E.

2. Repeat Step 1 to create a second panel. Feel free to use your own improvisational combination of pieces or a single piece of fabric for the other side. Make sure that the back panel is the same size as the front.

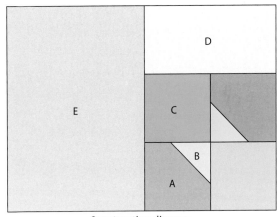

Construction diagram.
Complete panel measures 13.3 × 16.5cm (5¼″ × 6½″).

Sew the Pouch

1. The short side of the panels is the height of the pouch, and the long side is the width. Place the front and back panels good sides together, and sew along the sides and bottom, using a 1cm (⅜″) seam allowance. Leave the top edge unsewn. To give the pouch a boxy corner, fold the bottom corners in the shape of a triangle and sew across the corners 2cm (¾″) from the point to create a gusset. Turn the pouch right side out. *fig A*

2. Repeat Step 1 to sew together the lining. Leave an unsewn gap about 5cm (2″) in the centre of one of the side seams. Leave the good sides facing in. *fig B*

3. Grab the top band pieces. Place the exterior fabric and lining fabric together with good sides facing. Sew the two short ends together with a 1cm (⅜″) seam allowance. Turn it right side out. Press with an iron. Repeat with the other pair. *fig C*

4. Fold the top band lengthwise with the exterior facing out and the lining on the inside of the fold. Place the folded top band upside down along the unsewn top of the patchwork front. Sew the top band to the patchwork, making sure to sew as close as possible to the top edge. Repeat this with the second top band on the back side of the pouch. *fig D*

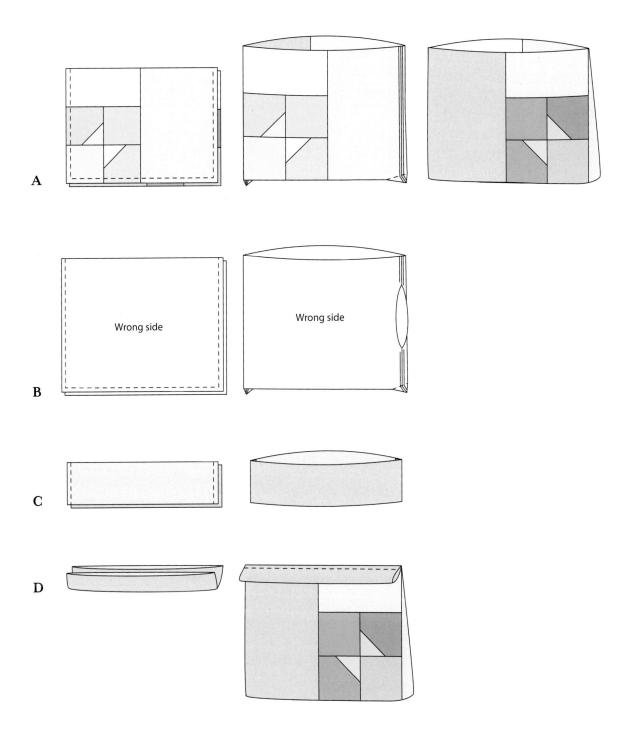

A

B

Wrong side

Wrong side

C

D

5. Place the outside of the pouch inside the lining with the good sides facing. Sew along the top edge with a 1cm (⅜″) seam allowance. *fig E*

6. Pull the the good sides of the pouch out through the unsewn gap on the side of the lining. Push the corners out so they are neat. Hand sew the gap in the lining closed with a blind stitch (see Stitch Directory, page 20). *fig F*

7. Using the sewing machine, sew a topstitch just underneath the top band. Topstitch along the whole top edge. This will make all the layers stay flat. *fig G*

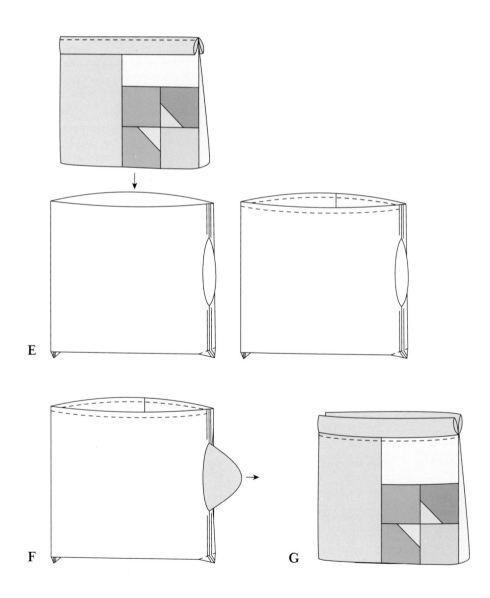

Inserting the Frame

1. Open one side of the squeeze/flex frame and slide each arm into and through each side of the top band. Close the squeeze/flex frame by inserting the pin into the slot and bending down the little tab with pliers.

Tote Bag

FINISHED BAG: 38 × 40 × 12cm (15˝ × 15¾˝ × 4¾˝)

Perfect as an errand tote or project bag, this bag has a wonderful front pocket that is made up of a patchwork of various remnants pieced together in an almost random fashion. The visual variety of the pocket really stands out from the neutral canvas and shows how much quilting or patchwork can transform an item.

FABRIC

1 yard (91.4cm) canvas 150cm (60″) wide

    Bag back 42 × 38cm (16½″ × 15″) E

    2 bag lining pieces 42 × 38cm (16½″ × 15″) G

    2 top drawstring panels 42 × 20cm (16½″ × 8″) H

    2 pocket side panels 11 × 38cm (4½″ × 15″) C

    Pocket lining 26 × 22cm (10¼″ × 8¾″) F

    Pocket back 26 × 29cm (10¼″ × 11½″) A

    Pocket bottom panel 26 × 11cm (10¼″ × 4½″) B

    Interior pocket panel 33 × 23cm (13″ × 9″) D

¼ yard (22.9cm) remnant and scrap fabric for patched pocket, to create a pieced panel 26 × 22cm (10¼″ × 8¾″)

ADDITIONAL MATERIALS

Two pieces webbing 2.5 × 62cm (1″ × 24½″) for straps

Two pieces cord 5mm × 130cm (5mm × 51″) for the drawstring

Water-soluble marker

Paper card to make templates (optional)

Safety pins or small appliqué pins

Sewing machine and thread

Scissors

Serger (optional)

Iron

Notes on Materials

I have chosen a natural canvas fabric for the body of the bag, but feel free to use something more lightweight combined with an interfacing to give it structure. I also kept to a neutral colour, but you're welcome to use coloured fabric instead.

My patchwork panel is made up of improvisationally pieced squares, rectangles, and part of a sawtooth star block. Use this final project as an opportunity to practise improvisational patchwork, use any samples or remnants you have left over, and create a bag that is truly your own. Feel free to use a pencil and paper to plan your design.

Stitch the Patchwork

1. Cut the patchwork fabric into shapes as desired. Stitch the patchwork together to make a panel 26 × 22cm (10¼″ × 8¾″). Press the seams flat. For more, see Putting Things Together (page 26).

2. Attach the pocket lining (F) to the patchwork by placing the pocket lining on top of the patchwork, good sides facing each other, and sewing along the top edge only with a 1cm (⅜″) seam allowance. Flip the lining over to the back of the patchwork so that the good sides are out. Align the bottom edges, and then sew a topstitch along the fold at the top edge.

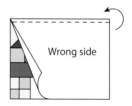

Wrong side

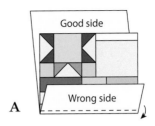

A

Sew the Tote Bag

1. Place the patched pocket, good side facing up, on top of the canvas for the pocket back (A), aligned along the 26cm (10¼″) bottom edge. Place the bottom pocket panel (B) on top of the pocket, good side down, aligning it along the bottom 26cm (10¼″) edge. Sew all layers together with a 1cm (⅜″) seam allowance. Flip the bottom canvas over, and sew two lines of topstitching along the seam. One row of stitching should be as close to the edge as possible, and the other should be 1cm (⅜″) away from the edge. *fig A*

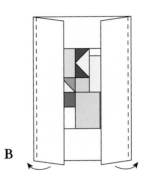

B

2. Again, with the patched pocket facing up, place one of the pocket side panels (C) on top, good side facing down, so that it is aligned with the side of the pocket and the top and bottom of the canvas pieces above and below the pocket. Sew all layers together with a 1cm (⅜″) seam allowance; then flip the side panel over and sew two lines of top stitching, as in Step 1. Repeat for the second side panel on the opposite side of the pocket. *fig B*

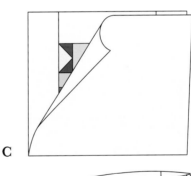

C

3. Place the bag's back canvas panel (E) on top of the pocket panel with good sides facing each other and all four edges aligned. Sew the sides and bottom together with a 1cm (⅜″) seam allowance. Then sew a 12cm (4¾″) gusset on both lower corners; to do this, fold the corners flat in the shape of a triangle and sew across the corners. Turn the bag right side out. *fig C*

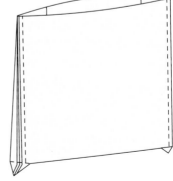

4. Sew a rolled hem along the long edge of the interior pocket panel (D). To do this, roll the edge over to the backside about 0.6cm (¼″), smooth it flat, and then fold another 1cm (⅜″) so that the raw edge is hidden. Sew along the edge of the hem through all layers with your sewing machine, or hand stitch with a blind stitch (see Stitch Directory, page 20).

Place the pocket on top of one of the lining panels (G), centred and about 10cm (4″) down from the top, and pin in place. Fold the edges under and sew around the remaining three sides. Add a second row of stitches. Leave the top seam open. Add a vertical seam in the middle if you want dividers in the pocket. *fig D*

5. Place the two bag lining panels (G) together, good sides facing, and sew along the two sides and the bottom with a 1cm (⅜″) seam allowance. Sew a 12cm (4¾″) gusset on each bottom corner. Leave the good sides facing in. Place the lining of the bag into the outside of the bag. Make sure to put the side with the interior pocket on the opposite side from the exterior pocket. Pin in place with the top edges aligned. *fig E*

6. Sew together the top drawstring panels (H) so that the bag can be cinched with a cord. If you'd like, serge the short sides of the panels prior to sewing, or just leave them with raw edges. Place the two panels together, aligned on all four sides. Sew halfway up the two short sides using a 1cm (⅜″) seam allowance. The short ends are now partially stitched together with a seam and an open slit. To finish the sides, fold the seam allowances over and continue the fold up along the unsewn slit. Using your sewing machine, sew the folded edge down on each side, reinforcing the point where the two sides meet by stitching back and forth a few times.

On the top of each panel, fold the edge over to the outside to make a rolled hem. To do this, roll the edge over to the backside about 0.6cm (¼″), and then fold again 2.5cm (1″) so that you have a space inside the hem for two drawstring cords. Sew along the edge of the hem with your sewing machine, or hand stitch with a blind stitch (see Stitch Directory, page 20). Leave the good sides facing in. *fig F*

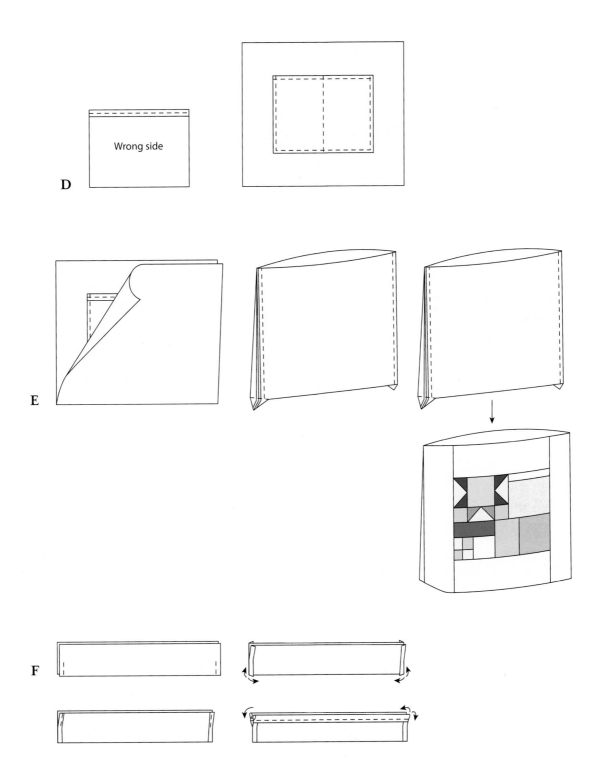

D

Wrong side

E

F

7. Slide the prepared top drawstring panels onto the exterior of the bag upside down, so that the bottom edges of the drawstring panels are aligned with the top edges of the bag and lining, good sides facing. On each side, place the two straps, also upside down, in between the layers of the drawstring panels and the bag bottom, approximately 9.5cm (3¾″) from the end seams. Let the strap ends extend about 2.5cm (1″) beyond the top edge of the bag. Sew around the entire top of the bag with 1cm (⅜″) seam allowance. *fig G*

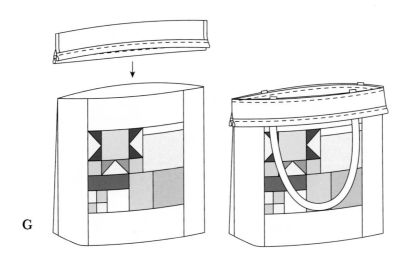

G

8. Bring the drawstring panels over the top edge and push them down into the bag, but keep the handles upright. Sew two rows of topstitching around the entire top of the bag. Make the first stitch close to the edge and the second one about 2.5cm (1″) below. *fig H*

9. Pull the drawstring panels up out of the bag, and feed the two cotton drawstrings through the slots from opposite sides. Tie the ends of the strings together with a knot. *fig I*

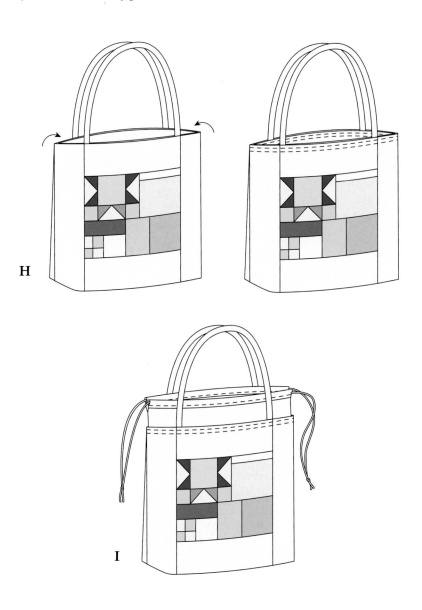

H

I

ABOUT THE AUTHOR

Arounna Khounnoraj is an artist and maker living in Canada, where she immigrated with her family from Laos at the age of four. Her education includes a master's degree in fine arts in sculpture and ceramics, but it was through subsequent art residencies that she found her current focus in fibre arts with an emphasis on surface design techniques and textile printing. In 2002, she, along with her husband, John Booth, cofounded bookhou, a multidisciplinary studio where Arounna furthered her interest in screen printing and block printing as a means of translating her drawings onto fabric. Her use of hand-drawn imagery and botanical references contributed to a full range of items such as home goods and personal accessories, including bags. Her use of natural materials, combined with her ever-expanding interest in various forms of stitchwork like embroidery and punch needle, gives her work all the qualities of handmade, slow design.

Arounna has collaborated with artists and manufacturers both locally and internationally. She has created two fabric collections with Free Spirit and is currently working on new textile designs for Kokka in Japan. She has also collaborated with Socksappeal and Roots Canada, creating products with her designs.

Arounna has complemented her studio work by teaching workshops on various techniques all over the globe and has expanded this work with a large social media presence, which includes her popular videos on stitching techniques, as well as her studio explorations. She has done online workshops for the past few years and has created teaching videos with The Crafter's Box and Creativebug.

Arounna's videos have helped to popularize a renewed interest in punch-needle techniques. In 2019, she published her first book, *Punch Needle: Master the Art of Punch Needling Accessories for You and Your Home*. In 2020, she released *Visible Mending: A Modern Guide to Darning, Stitching and Patching the Clothes You Love*, which introduced mending and the reuse of clothing as a personal and hands-on way to address issues of overconsumption and fast fashion in the textile industry. Her third book, *Embroidery: A Modern Guide to Botanical Embroidery*, was released in 2022.

Arounna currently lives in Toronto and Montreal, Canada. Her work can be found at bookhou.com and on Instagram @bookhou.